THE ART OF PERSUASION

EVERYTHING THEY NEVER TOLD YOU ABOUT THE
MANIPULATION OF EMOTIONS. A SPEED GUIDE TO
DISCOVER THE MIND OF OTHER PEOPLE AND
UNDERSTAND THEIR THOUGHTS

BRYAN COOPER

TABLE OF CONTENTS

PART ONE

Chapter 1 Start Hacking The Mind, Persuasion Techniques And Manipulation Techniques

The Basics Of Mind Reading

A high number of people aren't aware of mind reading, thought transference and how best to analyze people. Lately, scientists have been running studies and further hypothesis about the truth. Ignorance still shielded people into not believing such things as mind-reading ever existed. These beliefs made people so skeptical about any thinker that wants to employ these tools of reading people's minds.

The world keeps revolving and today we have a different application and thoughts towards the subject. This new science has come to stay with us as the world now revolves around several relationships and the art of reading intentions.

To read someone's mind, there are two possible facts to uphold - the instant change in the brain of the party suggesting and the respective change in the brain of the other party B who is the recipient of the proposed opinion. Between these two occurrences, there is supposed to be a pause to question whether to consider the suggestion of the mind. This has a lot to do with the sequence of thoughts and how they unfold.

The structure of the brain is so connected to conceive impulses as fast as it receives it which brings a connecting channel to what one believes and what it is. As brain nerves keep expanding as it sees any iota of reasoning, it is never right to say the brain reaches a limit for thinking. However, as the action of thought gets more tedious in deciding the way to follow, there are physical vibrations that show the extreme capabilities of reasoning.

With the strange outlook of assumptions and the bewildering stances of getting what the brain is interpreting, mind-reading occurs subconsciously. This belief brings the human closer to all tools of observation, hypothetical nuances and the feeble analysis that comes with reasoning.

As this takes a different shape in thinking, it is safe to say that the universe is about embracing the fashioned way of analyzing the mind, human behaviors and what is left behind as options. Doing this fortifies the mind into higher tasks of deciding the possibilities to rely on thereby justifying the judgment of the heart.

Non-verbal communication conveys in a split second and easily an individual's solace or distress in a given circumstance. An individual's outward appearance or position can alarm others to peril. For example, let's say someone opens the fridge and grabs a liter of soured milk. A bent articulation and eyes full of caution immediately send the message, "Don't drink that!" saving the first person from the disgusting experience of drinking soured milk.

An old piece of the mind called the limbic cerebrum is for the most part in charge of communicating implicit assumptions utilizing motion, facial changes, and wild eye-widening. Miniaturized scale articulations are momentary and pass on distinct emotions even in grown-ups who can buy and considerable control their outward appearances somewhat

Techniques Used in Mental Manipulation

Persuasion Technique

Persuasion is controlling the human mind without the knowledge of the manipulated party. This technique accesses your right mind, which is imaginative and creative, while the left side is rational and analytical. In persuasion, the perpetrator distracts your left brain and occupy it. It leaves you in an eyes-open altered state but still conscious, making you move from Beta awareness to Alpha. This technique is famous for politicians and lawyers.

Subliminal Programming

These are masked suggestions that can only be understood by your subconscious mind. They can be suggestions in audios, airbrushed visual suggestions, and flash images on your television quickly so that you do not consciously notice them. Some subliminal programming on audio makes suggestions on low volume. Your subconscious mind will notice these suggestions, but no one can monitor them even with equipment. The music we listen to can have a second voice behind it to program your mind. In 1984, a newsletter called Brain-Mind Bulletin that 99% of our activities are non-conscious.

Mass misuse - During mass meetings, the attendees go in and out of consciousness. If you have no idea, you cannot notice what is happening to you. It is a mental manipulation of the mass through vibrations. These vibrations produce Alpha, which makes the mass vulnerable. These make them accept any suggestion of the speaker as a command.

Vibrato - Vibrato is some effect installed on instrumental music or vocal, which makes people go in a distorted state of mind. In English history, some singers who had vibrato in their voices were not given chances to perform because of the effect they had on the public. Some listeners would have fantasies, mostly sexual fantasies.

Neurophone - Dr. Patrick Flanagan invented Neurophone. It is a device that can program your mind when it gets in contact with your skin. When this device gets in contact with your skin, you lose your sense and sight for a moment. It is because the skin has sensors for pain, touch, vibration, and heat. The message to manipulate your mind is played through Neurophone, which is connected and placed in the ceiling and no speakers. This message goes directly to the brain of the audience, and the manipulator can easily manipulate their mental state.

Medium for take-over - When you know how humans' function, you get the ability to control them. Medium take-over is happening in the televisions we watch. When people are put in a distorted state of mind, they function on the right brain, which releases brain opiates and makes you feel good, and you want it more. The broadcasts in our televisions induce the Alpha making us accept the broadcast easily. It makes viewers translate suggestions as commands. Every minute spent on watching television conditions us.

The Best Techniques of Persuasion

Before we dive deeper into the major facets of persuasion, we have to comprehend the meaning of persuasion. Persuasion refers to the psychological influence which affects the choice that an individual ought to make. With persuasion, an individual is often inclined to make you buy his or her school of thought in a bid to change your thought process. To effectively achieve persuasion, there are a number of things that need to be kept in mind. When we go beyond the natural human framework and get a grasp of what moves others, then we are positioned to achieve effective persuasion. This is because you are aware of the pressure points and how best to manipulate them.

When exploiting the art of persuasion, there are various pointers that can come in handy:

Mimicking

As human beings of reason, we tend to vary from one individual to another. The diversity of this is what makes us appear in the discrepancy of others. You will find that as individuals, we are more drawn to be warm and welcoming to those people who exhibit the same characteristics as us. It could be a physical trait or just the way an individual carry themselves. When an individual has the feelings of. liking towards someone, he or she is in a position to be swayed by your influence.

In a bid to elaborate on this technique, we are going to employ the use of this scenario. In the hotel industry, especially in the most advanced and high-end ones, you will find that the allocation of a waiter is dependent on the customer. High-end hotels in the industry have high customer feedback and thus they tend to treat their clients in a manner that suggests so. A client, for instance, would be allocated a particular type of waiter who matches their description. For instance, French waiters are renowned for their exquisite service. Putting the client first is at the top of the list when it comes to this particular field. Many professionals have succeeded in this area owing to the manner in which they treated clients. This is because of the clients are the main source of business. Putting the client into consideration goes a notch higher to even saying the exact words that the client has said. With this, they are able to gather that you have aptly decoded what they meant.

In order to achieve this particular technique, an individual ought to do a number of things. First, he or she may consider doing in-depth research into the particular field of the question in order to see to it that what is required of them. Before you can achieve persuasion by the use of this technique, one ought to be well versed with the individual that he or she ought to persuade. This type of expertise should be keen enough to make sure that it elicits major points that may come in handy during the process of persuasion.

Social Proof

When it comes to persuasion, social proof has repeatedly proven its dominance. Social proof refers to the process by which an individual's feelings and thought process are affected by the way other people have reacted to the same issue. An individual who is the persuader, draw his or her basis from the acts that others have engaged in time and again. It could be the norm. With human beings, the danger that occurs is the feeling of wanting to be associated with a group of people. Humans crave a sense of belonging to a group and this is what puts them at risk of being influenced easily.

Employing social proof when persuading an individual will mean that you have a basis of a norm that has been used repeatedly by the people whom we consider to be in the same class. This basis must be something that most people engage in. Take, for instance, there are newbies in the estate who are looking for service providers. This newbie would first be inclined to know what other people in the estate are using. Although they might not settle on the same option as the rest of the estate, this will be somewhat a buildup on to what choice they may choose to settle upon. Rather they may end up embracing what others have used. The trick lies whereby you ought to create a distinction in the manner in which an individual sees himself or herself as per against others. You will only achieve persuasion by convincing this individual that the desired option is one that has been embraced by a large group of individuals.

Reciprocity

When it comes to this technique, one needs to understand that a good deed was done to another individual no matter how remote, tends to go a long way. "Reciprocity" refers to the process by which an individual is able to respond to a good deed by performing a good deed in return. With this type of technique, we will find that most people fail to notice at its onset not until you are obligated to return the favor. In the world today, it is almost as rare as the sun rising from the west as it is to find someone who will extend warmness and care towards you. Except for the people to whom we are closely related, we tend to feel differently when an individual who is not even in our circle of friendship extends warm-hearted feelings.

Chapter 2 Dark Persuasion

Persuasion is an interesting topic. There are lots of persuasions that are considered just fine in society. They are acceptable, and even some people hold jobs where they will spend a lot of time trying to persuade others. Any attempt by one person to influence someone else to do some action can be persuasion. A salesperson at a car dealership is using persuasion because they try to persuade someone to purchase a new vehicle. This isn't seen as something sinister or bad. The difference here is that this persuasion and other similar examples of persuasion benefit both parties. The car dealer makes a sale and some money, and the "victim" is going to get a new vehicle.

There are a lot of legitimate types of persuasion that aren't considered part of dark psychology. The car dealer above is an example. If a negotiator uses their skills to persuade a terrorist to let their hostage go, this is a good form of persuasion. If you convince someone to come along to an event that they will enjoy, then this is a good form of persuasion. This type of persuasion is seen as positive persuasion. But then, what would count as dark persuasion?

Understanding Dark Persuasion

The first difference you will notice between positive and dark persuasion is the motive behind it. Positive persuasion is used in order to encourage someone to complete an action that isn't going to cause them any harm. In some cases, such as with the negotiator saving a hostage, this persuasion can be used to help save lives.

But with dark persuasion, there isn't really any form of moral motive. The motive is usually amoral, and often immoral. If positive persuasion is understood as a way to help people help themselves, then dark persuasion is more of the process of making people act against their own self-interest. Sometimes, people are going to do these actions begrudgingly, knowing that they are probably not making the right choice, but they do it because they are eager to stop the incessant persuasion efforts. In other cases, the best dark persuader is going to make their victim think that they acted wisely, but the victim is actually doing the opposite in that case.

So, what are the motivations for someone who is a dark persuader? This is going to depend on the situation and the individual who is doing the persuading. Some people like to persuade their victims in order to serve their own self-interests. Others are going to act through with the intention just to cause some harm to the other person. In some cases, the persuader is not going to really benefit from darkly persuading their victim, but they do so because they want to inflict pain on the other person. And still, others enjoy the control that this kind of persuasion gives to them.

You will also find that the outcome you get from dark persuasion is going to differ from what happens with positive persuasion.

The benefit goes to the person who is being persuaded.

There is a win/win benefit for the persuaded and the persuader.

There is a mutual benefit for the person who is persuaded and a third party.

All of these outcomes are good because they will involve a positive result for the person who is being persuaded. Sometimes, there will be others who benefit from these actions. But out of all three situations, the persuaded party is always going to benefit.

With dark persuasion, the outcome is going to be very different. The persuader is the one who will always benefit when they exercise their need for influence or control. The one who is being persuaded often goes against what is in their self-interest when they listen, and they are not going to benefit from all this dark persuasion.

In addition, the most skilled dark persuaders are not only able to cause some harm to their victims while also benefiting themselves, but they could also end up harming others in the process.

Unmasking the Dark Persuader

At this point, you may be curious about who is using these dark methods of persuasion. Are there actually people out there who are interested in using this kind of persuasion and using it against others to cause harm? The main characteristics of a dark persuader are either an indifference toward or an inability to care about how persuasion is going to impact others. Such people who use this kind of persuasion are going to be often narcissistic and will see their own needs as more important than the needs of others. They may even be sociopathic and unable to grasp the idea of someone else's emotions.

Many times, this kind of dark persuasion is going to show up in a relationship. Often one but sometimes both partners are going to be inclined towards trying to use dark persuasion on each other. If these attempts are persistent and endure, then this type of relationship is going to be classified as psychologically abusive, and that is not healthy for the victim in that relationship. Often, they will not realize that there is something going on or that they are darkly persuaded until it is too late, and they are stuck there.

There are many examples of using this kind of dark persuasion in a relationship. If one partner stops the other partner from taking a new job opportunity or doesn't allow them to go out with friends, then this could be an example of dark persuasion. The dark persuader will work to convince the victim that they are acting in a way that is best for the relationship. In reality, the victim is going through a process that harms them and the relationship.

So, how exactly is a dark persuader able to use this idea in order to carry out their wishes? There are a few different types of tactics that a dark manipulator is going to use, but some of the most common options include:

The Long Con

The first method that we are going to look at is the Long Con. This method is kind of slow and drawn out, but it can be really effective because it takes so long and is hard to recognize or even pinpoint when something went wrong. One of the main reasons that some people have the ability to resist persuasion is because they feel that they are being pressured by the other person, and this can make them back off. If they feel that there is a lack of rapport or trust with the person who is trying to persuade them, they will steer clear as well. The Long Con is so effective because they are able to overcome these main problems and give the persuader exactly what they want.

The Long Con is going to involve the dark persuader to take their time, working to earn the trust of their victim. They are going to take some time to befriend the victim and make sure that their victim trusts and likes them. This is going to be achieved by the persuader with artificial rapport building, which sometimes seems excessive, and other techniques that will help to increase the comfort levels between the persuader and their victim.

As soon as the persuader sees that the victim is properly readied psychologically, the persuader is going to begin their attempts. They may start out with some insincere positive persuasion. The persuader is going to lead their victim into making a choice or doing some action that will actually benefit the persuader. This is going to serve the persuader in two ways. First, the victim starts to become used to persuasion by that persuader. The second is that the victim is going to start making that mental association between a positive outcome and the persuasion.

The Long Con is going to take a long period of time to complete because the persuader doesn't want to make it too obvious what they are doing. An example of this is a victim who is a recently widowed lady who is vulnerable because of her age and from their bereavement. After her loss, a man starts to befriend her. This man may be someone she knows from church or even a relative. He starts to spend more time with her, showing immense kindness and patience, and it doesn't take too long for her guard to drop when he comes around.

Then this man starts to carry out some smaller acts of positive persuasion that we talked about before. He may advise her of a better bank account to use or a better way to reduce any monthly bills. The victim is going to appreciate these efforts and the fact that the man is trying to help her, and she takes the advice.

Over some time, the man then tries to use some dark persuasion. He may try to persuade her to let him invest some of her money. She obliges because of the positive persuasion that was used in the past. Of course, the man is going to work to take everything he can get from her. If the manipulator is skilled enough, she may feel that he actually tried to help her, but the money is lost because he just ran into some bad luck with the investment. This is how far dark persuasion can go.

Graduality

Often when we hear about acts of dark persuasion, it seems impossible and unbelievable. What they fail to realize is that this dark persuasion isn't ever going to be a big or a sudden request that comes out of nowhere. Dark persuasion is more like a staircase. The dark persuader is never going to ask the victim to do something big and dramatic the first time they meet. Instead, they will have the victim take one step at a time.

When the manipulator has the target only go one step at a time, the whole process seems like less of a big deal. Before the victim knows it, they have already gone a long way down, and the persuader isn't likely to let them leave or come back up again.

Let's take an example of how this process is going to look in real life. Let's say that there is a criminal who wanted to make it so that someone else committed the crimes for them. Gang bosses, cult leaders, and even Charles Manson did this exact same thing.

This criminal wouldn't dream of beginning the process by asking their victim to murder for them. This would send out a red flag, and no one in their right minds would willingly go out and kill for someone they barely know. Instead, the criminal would start out by having the victim do something small, like a petty crime, or simply hiding a weapon for them. Something that isn't that big of a deal for the victim, at least in comparison.

Over time, the acts that the manipulator is able to persuade their victim to do will become more severe. And since they did the smaller crimes, the persuader now has the unseen leverage of holding some of those smaller misdeeds over the victim, kind of like for blackmail.

Before the victim knows it, they are going to feel like they are in too deep. They will then be persuaded to carry out some of the most shocking crimes. And often, by this point, they will do it because they feel like they have no other choice.

Dark persuaders are going to be experts at using this graduality to help increase the severity of their persuasion over time. They know that no victim would be willing to jump the canyon or do the big crime or misdeed right away. So, the persuader works to build a bridge to get there. By the time the victim sees how far in they are, it is too late to turn back.

Chapter 3 The Power Of Persuasion

There are many times when the human mind is pretty easy to influence, but it does take a certain set of skills to get people to stop and listen to you. Not everyone is good with influence and persuasion, though. They can talk all day and would not be able to convince others to do what they want. On the other hand, there are those who could persuade anyone to do what they want, even if they had just met this person for the first time. Knowing how to work with these skills will make it easier for you to recognize a manipulator and be better prepared to avoid them if needed.

The first thing that we need to look at is what persuasion is. Persuasion is simply the process or action taken by a person or a group of people when they want to cause something to change. This could be in relation to another human being and something that changes in their inner mental systems or their external behavior patterns.

The act of persuasion, when it is done in the proper way, can sometimes create something new within the person, or it can just modify something that is already present in their minds. There are actually three different parts that come with the process of persuasion including:

- The communicator or other source of the persuasion
- The persuasive nature of the appeal
- The audience or the target person of the appeal

It is important that all three elements are taken into consideration before you try to do any form of persuasion on your own. You can just look around at the people who are in your life, and you will probably be able to see some types of persuasion happening all over the place.

Experts say that people who are good leaders and who have good persuasion powers will utilize the following techniques to help them be successful:

- Exchanging
- Stating
- Legitimizing
- Logical persuasion
- Appealing to value
- Modeling
- Alliance building
- Consulting
- Socializing
- Appealing to a relationship

The above options are all positive ways that you can use persuasion to your advantage. Most people will be amenable to these happening. But on the other side, there are four negative tactics of persuasion that you can do as well. These would include options like manipulating, avoiding, intimidating, and threatening. These negative tactics will be easier for the target to recognize, which is why most manipulators will avoid using them if possible.

Now, you can use some of the tactics above, but according to psychologist Robert Cialdini, there are six major principles of persuasion that can help you to get the results that you want without the target being able to notice what is going on. Let us take a look at these six weapons and how they can be effective.

The six weapons of influence

Reciprocity

The first principle of persuasion that you can use is known as reciprocity. This is based on the idea that when you offer something to someone, they will feel a bit indebted to you and will want to reciprocate it back. Humans are wired to be this way to survive. For the manipulator to use this option, they will make sure that they are doing some kind of favor for their target. Whether that is paying them some compliments, giving them a ride to work, helping out with a big project or getting them out of trouble. Once the favor is done, the target will feel like they owe a debt to the manipulator. The manipulator will then be able to ask for something, and it will be really hard for the target to say no.

Commitment and consistency

It is in the nature of humans to settle for what is already tried and tested in the mind. Most of us have a mental image of who we are and how things should be. And most people are not going to be willing to experiment, so they will keep on acting the way that they did in the past. So, to get them to work with this principle and do what you want, you first need to get them to commit to something. The steps that you would need to follow to get your target to do what you want through commitment and consistency include:

• Start out with something small. You can ask the target to do something small, something that is easier to manage the change, before they start to integrate it more into their personality and get hooked on the habit.

• You can get the target to accept something publicly so that they will feel more obligated to see it through.

• Reward the target when they can stick to the course. Rewards will be able to help strengthen the interest of the target in the course of action that you want them to do.

Social proof

This is another one that will rely on the human tendency, and it relies on the fact that people place a lot of value and trust in other people and in their opinions on things that we have not tried yet. This can be truer if the information comes from a close friend or a person who is perceived as the expert. It is impossible to try out everything in life and having to rely on others can put us at a disadvantage. This means that we need to find a reliable source to help us get started. A manipulator may be able to get someone to do something by acting as a close friend or an expert. They are able to get the target to try out a course of action because they have positioned themselves as the one who knows the most about the situation or the action.

Likeability

We all know that it is easy to feel attracted to a certain set of people. This can extend to friends and family members as well. So, if you would like to get others to like you and be open to persuasion from you, you first need to figure out how to go from an acquaintance to a friend. This will work similarly to the reciprocity that we talked about earlier, but some of the basic steps that you will need to follow to make this work include:

● The attraction phase: You need to make sure that there is something about you that instantly draws the other person to you.

● Make yourself relatable: People are more likely to be drawn to you if you are relatable to them in some way. It is also easier to influence another person if they consider you their friend.

● Communicate like a friend: Even if the two of you are not quite friends yet, you will be able to make use of the right communication skills so that the target will associate you as a friend.

● Make it look like you are both in the same groups and that you are fighting for the same causes: This can make it easier to establish a rapport with them.

Authority

If you want to make sure that you can influence another person, then you need to dress and act the part. This means that you should wear clothes, as well as accessories, that will help you look like you are the one in command. Some of the ways that you can do this include:

● Wear clothes that are befitting to what people will perceive an authoritative figure would wear.

● When you communicate with the target, you need to do so in a commanding fashion.

● Make sure that you can use the lexicon and the language of experts in that field.

When you can position yourself as the authority figure, people will look to you for the answers that they need. It does not matter how well they know you or not. You will have a great opportunity to influence them the way that you want them to behave.

Scarcity

The last weapon that you can use for persuasion is known as scarcity. Humans like the idea of being exclusive and are drawn to anything that they are not necessarily able to find anywhere else. When you make something exclusive, you have a chance of making it appear more valuable. People are also going to become fearful when something they desire starts to disappear. This whole idea is part of the supply and demand principle. If you have something that is abundant, then it will be perceived as having a lower value and cheap. But if it is rare, then it must have a higher value and be more expensive.

This can work for human beings and for products in the same way. Some things that you should keep in mind when you want to use the scarcity principle with persuasion include:

- Always imply that the thing you are offering is not going to be available to the target anywhere else.

- If you can, it is a good idea to implement a countdown timer on what you are offering. This gives a physical indicator to the target that what you are offering is truly going to disappear.

- You should never go back on the stipulations that you said in the beginning. You need to make sure that the target knows that what you offered is scarce, or this method is not going to work very well.

All of these principles can be effective ways for you to be able to use persuasion to manipulate your target. It is important to learn how to use them all and to do so in a covert way so that your target is not able to realize what you are doing. When you are successful with bringing all of this together, you are sure to get the results that you want each time.

Chapter 4 The Importance Of Body Language

Dominance

Body language is a key part of displaying dominance, no matter the context. When a person enters the room, people consciously and subconsciously make judgments about that person based on what they see, how they hold themselves, and other subtle cues of nonverbal communication.

Katie enters a room, and her head is held high. She is not staring at the floor; she is making eye contact with the people she passes by and offering a slight nod and a grin as a greeting. Her posture is erect, with her shoulder back, and her stride is wide and confident. There is a slight sway to her hips that seems natural, and her arms swing freely at her sides. She has yet to actually speak to anyone, but you can form a pretty clear picture of what this person looks like as she enters the room. What is her body language communicating to you?

If you can form some kind of picture based on this description, there should be several adjectives that might come to mind describing her based on this nonverbal evidence. The first, as hinted at in the description, might be confidence. When someone holds themselves erect with their shoulders back, it tells people around her that she is not hiding from them and that she is confident enough to be on full display and to acknowledge and confront anyone she comes across, hence, the direct eye contact and brief greetings. And the higher the chin, the more the message moves across the confidence territory into the realm of dominance.

To assume and display dominance is to carry yourself in a way that does not connote fear or trepidation. The free swing of the arms and long strides suggests that she is not concerned with getting in anyone's way, and there is an unspoken expectation that people will get out of hers if need be.

Let us say Katie moves into one of the main offices, and there, she is awaited by a few powerful people who are meeting her for the first time. Now, we're ready for the handshake.

The handshake can actually say a lot more than most people know to look for, but it is common knowledge in the realm of power and money and politics that how you choose to shake someone's hand can be a strong signal to a person's attitude, as well as their perception of the person with whom they are shaking hands.

The way to signal a position of dominance involves shaking hands in a way that your hand is on top with the palm facing down. This places the other's hand in the subservient position or with the palm facing up. The grip and pressure which the person doing a handshake chooses to employ also send a message about dominance. Politicians who are constantly being photographed as they shake hands with other leaders and political figures might make special efforts to convey dominance by shaking hands in this position and making sure their hand is sending a strong signal to those who know what it means.

Katie chooses, however, to shake hands in a balanced way that does not assume dominance but instead orients the position of hands as to be equal with palms facing each other. This sends a non-threatening message of balance and a willingness to cooperate with another. It is smart to avoid intimidating or using aggressive behaviors in a situation where you want to form a working relationship based on trust and mutual benefit. Katie also is careful to smile and directly address the people she is meeting with eye contact and attentiveness. This should echo back to the first instances in which we examined how attentiveness, listening, and active engagement with a speaker sends the signal that you are interested and invested in what the subject is saying. From a broad point of view, we can say that Katie practices dominance and strong leadership when she is in front of her employees, and she likes to cultivate a balanced working relationship with higher-ups and colleagues of equal stature within the business.

There are certainly much more overt ways to assume dominance, such as outright aggression, and there are also very subtle, covert ways, such as in the instance of a young professional gradually taking over a room and winning the hearts of those whom he might later utilize to his advantage. The alpha then operates as the individual on top until another comes along who wants to take the position for himself, and the alpha is challenged.

Seduction

Seduction is another major category in which body language plays an especially vital role, both on the part of the person trying to seduce and his subject.

The reading of body language comes into play in this scenario as soon as the seducer makes his approach. From the moment the target acknowledges the seducer, she begins sending signals, which are both conscious and subconscious messages that will either reinforce the efficacy of the seducer's tactics or give him warning signs that his target is not as open to suggestion as he'd thought at first. Let's look at some examples.

The seducer approaches from behind the subject, who may be standing and listening to some music about to begin at a bar. When the approach happens, the target must turn her body to orient herself to the speaker if she is acknowledging the approach and willingness to engage. The seducer then examines how much of her body begins orienting toward him, and how much she is responding by keeping her orientation pointed away from the seducer. If she fully engages and turns to meet and look the seducer head-on, this is a strong signal that the lady is amenable to the interaction and is a strong positive sign that the seducer has chosen the right target for his intentions. On the other hand, if the target remains facing toward the stage and/or does not move to orient any part of her body toward the seducer, then she is sending a strong signal that she is completely uninterested in an interaction at that moment. This could be motivated by a variety of different reasons, but the seducer would usually abandon his approach and perhaps try again a little later; otherwise, he may simply move on to different target entirely.

The seducer pays attention to every movement and mannerism the target makes as he is engaging with her. The trick for successful interaction and seduction, however, is not to appear as if he is trying so hard to read her thoughts through her behaviors and nonverbal communication. An attempt at seduction, for example, which is accompanied by lots of staring at the target's body instead of her face, is certainly not going to go over well, as the seducer's intentions are all but being broadcast by his behavior and areas of attention.

The skilled seducer will be able to multitask as he listens to the target's words and pays attention to nonverbal cues as much as possible, without seeming like this is what he's doing. The seducer must come off as comfortable, friendly, and nonthreatening. The idea is to ignite some kind of attraction in whatever form he can. Once this is accomplished, he can begin playfully moving in as he exploits this newfound weakness. Positive body language cues that will often signal to the seducer that he is progressing well include smiling and giggling while keeping the body oriented toward the seducer. Women who are simply pretending to be comfortable and engage will often smile and giggle playfully, but the orientation of their bodies will give away their anxiety. The seducer would likely not move forward in this situation until he can inspire a little more comfort into the interaction. However, as the seducer persists, he also runs the risk of intensifying the anxiety, as the target may or may not be experiencing a gut instinct to stay away or get out of the situation. This can be a powerful tool on the part of the target if she is able to really pay attention and listen to her instincts when she feels something is a bit off.

As the seducer finds a target and is able to get some positive signals, he will use his own powers in the form of nonverbal communication to inspire attraction and interest. Flattery can be utilized in ways other than direct verbal communication. A seducer who wants to introduce just a bit of flirtation and sexual interest might let the target catch him looking briefly over her as he then quickly returns to face her. This tells her a lot of different things about the seducer, and if played correctly, it will work to the seducer's advantage if the signal comes off as playful and flirtatious without getting into creepy territory.

There is a balance to all of these behaviors and interaction, and the same methods may work differently based on the personality and demeanor of the target. This is why practiced seducers will zero in on specific types who more often respond positively to such advances.

Chapter 5 Sociopathy

Psychopathy and sociopathy are 2 personality conditions typically connected to serial killers or lawbreakers. In truth, though, there is so much more to psychopaths and sociopaths than meets the eye. In this segment, you will discover the true nature of the condition and the people who have it.

By the end of this segment, you should have a clear grasp of what causes psychopathy and what are the clear indicators that a person is a psychopath. More importantly, this segment will teach you how to stop being manipulated by one

. What and Who Is a Psychopath?

Psychopaths have gotten a lot of attention over the years, but extremely little information today is accurate. Considered as a character disorder, psychopaths are often seen as cold-blooded serial killers or those who have the prospective to become serial killers. This is not unexpected, thinking about how among the most popular serial killers today, Ted Bundy, is called as a psychopath. Still, others may argue that he is a sociopath instead.

Psychopaths versus Sociopaths.

These 2 terms are usually interchangeable, but there's actually a significant difference between these them. While the science is still not precise, studies have limited distinctions among the 2:

Regarding Cause.

It is normally accepted that psychopaths are born and not made. It is viewed as a hereditary quality, pursuant to a Minnesota Research study about the condition. On the other hand, sociopaths are made and not born. Sociopath propensities normally happen as a result of environmental factors that seriously affected an individual's frame of mind. It can be anything from the early loss of mom and dad to rejection by an enjoyed one.

Regarding Education.

While the condition is not a sign of intelligence, psychopaths typically have a pretty good career and are well-educated. In contrast, sociopaths are typically not able to hold down a stable job. It is also not likely that they have reached tertiary education. Of course, there are certain exceptions to this.

Regarding Conscience/Empathy.

Psychopaths are generally accepted to have no conscience and lack empathy. This is maybe the most defining attribute of a psychopath. On the other hand, a sociopath has little empathy. They have a conscience, but this is not exercised greatly. As a result, psychopaths form no attachments (although they may act a lot like they do) while sociopaths form little attachments to certain groups or individuals.

As to Conduct.

Psychopaths work out outstanding control in their own person and try to extend this to their surroundings. They are known to be highly manipulative as opposed to sociopaths that struggle with erratic behavior. Sociopaths are more likely to be aggressive and violent.

As to Criminal offense.

Keep in mind that being a psychopath/sociopath is not tantamount to be a criminal. Those who do fall into a life of criminal offense, though, tend to follow a general pattern for their acts. Psychopaths are careful and plans ahead, taking calculated risks and guaranteeing that the evidence is minimized, if not wiped tidy completely. Sociopaths are more out of control and tend to commit violent/physical crimes. Nowadays, psychopaths are more tailored toward organized crime, fraud plans, and the like.

Psychopath versus Narcissist.

Many individuals make the error of using these two terms interchangeably. There's actually a significant distinction between the 2 in that all psychopaths are narcissists but not all narcissists are psychopaths. Narcissism is a personality condition recognized by DSM (DMS-5) or the Diagnostic and Statistical Handbook of Mental Illness. It is defined by a grand sense of self-importance and a real need for extreme affection from other ones. Narcissists may also do not have empathy and believe that they are entitled to tons of things in life-- even if they do not necessarily work for the same. Narcissists often daydream about holding severe amounts of cash, power, control, charm, success, and so on. They believe that they are unique and thus should have to be looked up to by others.

A narcissist is not always a psychopath, since some of the qualities of the psychopath might not exist in a narcissist. Nevertheless, narcissism is an crucial attribute of a psychopath.

The 'degree' of narcissism also matters. Psychopaths typically fall within the extreme scale of self-grandiosity while some narcissists aren't as extreme in their belief of self-importance.

Psychopath versus Antisocial Personality Disorder.

Despite the obvious popularity of the terms psychopath and sociopath, it is fascinating to note that both character disorders aren't pointed out in the Diagnostic and Statistical Manual of Mental Illness. The acknowledged mental disorder that is closest to the definition of a psychopath is Antisocial Personality Condition. Regarding medical diagnosis nevertheless, psychiatrists do not identify an Antisocial Personality Disorder without a previous diagnosis of conduct condition. Thus, specialists usually make use of "Antisocial Character Disorder" instead of psychopath.

False Concepts About Psychopaths.

Since psychopaths are typically incorrect for serial killers, it's best to first get the myths out of the way. Here are some of the things you might have become aware of psychopaths but aren't entirely real:

Psychopaths Are Insane.

Psychopaths aren't insane. They work perfectly well within society's limits but is separated in their way of thinking. Many psychopaths are actually upstanding members of society or have managed to make a success out of their lives.

Psychopaths Are Wrongdoers.

A big part of psychopaths ends up as lawbreakers due to their inability to manage or effectively manage impulses and the consistent need for stimulation. As you'll learn later, though, criminal offense as a profession is just one of the options a psychopath has for work. There are presently jobs available that naturally draw in a psychopath and a lot of these are perfectly acceptable and even celebrated within society.

You're Either a Psychopath or You Aren't.

Do not expect that all psychopaths are a lot like Hannibal or Ted Bundy. Psychopathy actually exists on a spectrum, which means that while some characteristics of a psychopath are strong, some might be weak and therefore easily managed. In fact, research studies have shown that a lot of the past United States presidents have a level of boldness and assertiveness comparable to that of psychopathy. It must be kept in mind that this assertiveness is a crucial factor in what made them presidents.

You Can Self Really Diagnose Psychopathy.

While there are definitely a ton of online tests to help identify psychopathy, none of these are legitimate. For a correct diagnosis, people will have to go through a legitimate physician for personality disorders. Usually, it takes more than just a survey to detect psychopathy. Nowadays, a brain scan can be made to better track the brain's response when asked questions.

Psychopaths are Dangerous.

While a lot of the psychopath traits are negative, this does not immediately make them unsafe or violent. Be aware, though, that your mental health might be at threat, since psychopaths can quickly break down a person's confidence and self-esteem. If you feel as though you're at risk when with a psychopath, it's usually best to just move from them.

Signs and Characteristics of a Psychopath

The reason that these two-character conditions are typically interchanged, is as the standard characteristics of the two are remarkably similar. However, there are certain attributes that are unique to the psychopath. We'll talk about the characteristics that are unique in psychopaths along with those common with sociopaths. There's typically a 20-point character basis that experts use to check--

but keep in mind that a best rating is not necessary for a medical diagnosis. Some validated psychopaths do not have some characteristics-- but there are some that are never ever gone from the list.

Lack of Empathy/Remorse/Guilt

This is the most defining characteristic of a psychopath. Thus, it can be said that ALL psychopaths lack compassion. Empathy is the ability to get in touch with people and put yourself in their position so that you can have compassion with them on an emotional level. Compassion is the reason that people donate food to the homeless, say sorry after a mistake, and feel bad for doing something very wrong. It is the ability to recognize real pain in somebody-- and psychopaths do not have this ability. For this reason, psychopaths are mainly incapable of connecting with people or creating relationships. Note, though, that this is an internal characteristic and most psychopaths are smart adequate to fake compassion.

Lying Pathologically

Psychopaths are also pathological phonies in that they have this compulsive need to lie in order to suit their own ends. Sometimes, there isn't even any great reason for the lie as long as they find it practical to provide. Psychopaths can be rather skilled in their lies, particularly when it is part of their grand scheme. Being careful, some of their lies are well-thought of and thus hard to identify.

Superficial Appeal

Of all the qualities of psychopaths, beauty is maybe the most unexpected among all. Psychopaths have the fantastic ability to coax people into their point of view, radiating an appeal that can be appealing for most people. While some psychopaths are not as achieved in faking the genuineness of their charm, there are those that are more than capable of fooling the public. Ted Bundy, infamous serial killer and psychopath was so skilled in exercising charm that ladies happily supported him during his trial for murder.

Manipulative

Together with charm is their capability to control people. Combine this with their lying capability and psychopaths can be exceptional puppet masters. In simple fact, studies show that there are tons of psychopaths in top-fields of business and politics, 2 professions that require a certain mix of appeal for success.

Promiscuous Conduct

Their lack of guilt or remorse makes it simple for psychopaths to exceed societal limits without thinking twice about it. This is why a lot of psychopaths have no issue remaining in some relationships at once-- even if they are already married. They are promiscuous and their manipulative character makes it simple for them to manage several relationships at one time.

Inflated Sense of Self Worth

They actually believe that they are better than other ones in practically every element, which is a conceited trait. Psychopaths need to be smarter than everyone else, stronger than everyone else, make more than everybody else, drive a better car, and so on. They are of the opinion that they are always right and will for that reason have a hard time accepting errors or criticisms.

Blaming Others

Since psychopaths really believe that they can never be really wrong, it makes a lot of sense for them that another person slipped up. They always blame other ones and never accept duties for mistakes or issues. On the flipside, if something good happens, they fast to take credit.

Continuous Need for Stimulation

Research studies have shown that psychopaths have a consistent need for stimulation. This can be connected to the fact that they do not have compassion and therefore do not feel the same low and high of emotions related to relationships. Psychopaths need a much different way in which to promote their senses. They have the tendency to lock down on a particular stimulation and pursue it till they are satisfied. An issue is that, much like druggie, some psychopaths might need a larger fix each time for stimulation to happen. This is why psychopaths who are also killers typically reach this level by steps. Other criminal behavior happens right before they commit murder.

Chapter 6 The Levels Of Consciousness

Freud's theory subdivides the human mind into three levels of consciousness. These levels play a major role in influencing people. The three levels are:

The conscious mind

The subconscious mind

The unconscious mind

Each of these three contributes a certain percentage to reality.

The conscious mind

Consciousness can be defined as the state of being aware of something. It refers to the ability to conceive something like an event or activity in the mind and recalling it after it has already taken place. From figure 1 above, it is estimated that only 10% of the human brain constitutes the conscious mind.

Some of the common functions of the conscious mind are to:

Control a person's focus or concentration for the short-term memory

Imagine things that are not real

Collect and process data

Identify and make a comparison between patterns

Respond to situations in a thoughtful way

Make decisions

Give orders

This segment of the mind works in the form of a scanner. It helps you to identify or understand events and activities trigger the reaction and store the occurrences related to the event in the subconscious or unconscious segment of the mind. People are always aware of every activity that goes on in their conscious mind.

The subconscious mind

This is the place where memories that you need to remember quickly are stored. Such memories may be things like your identity card or telephone number. It acts as a storage place for the information you use on a daily basis. This information is what forms your habits, behavioral patterns, and feelings.

The subconscious mind works the same way as a computer's random-access memory. It is where dreams come from as well as the knowledge required to do some of the things you are used to.

The unconscious mind

This is the level that holds all the past memories and experiences. It acts as a storage place for most of the memories that are no longer important, and those, which are almost being forgotten. These memories and experiences also contribute a great deal to a person's behaviors, habits, and beliefs.

The unconscious mind is directly connected to the subconscious mind. However, the unconscious mind is a collection of all the habits, memories and behaviors of a person. It is like a reservoir that contains all the emotions you have been collecting since birth.

The unconscious mind accounts for between 30 to 40 percent of the human brain. It plays a very essential role yet it is mostly inaccessible. As an individual, you may fail to understand what goes on at this level of the mind. The major roles of the unconscious mind are:

Performs most of the activities within the body – these include sleeping, breathing, heartbeat, controlling the temperature and many other activities that do not require your input

Protects you by keeping you to what you are familiar with and shielding you from carrying out some uncomfortable actions and decisions

Is the source of human emotions

It is also the source of creativity and imagination skills

It is the place where habits are made and controlled

Stores long-term memories

Besides these functions, the unconscious mind also takes instructions from the conscious mind. It triggers you to react towards threats. One characteristic of the unconscious mind that you should take note of is that it does not make any judgments. This means that you cannot depend on it when you need to make a choice between things that are good and those that are bad. It only accepts instructions from the conscious mind and causes the person to automatically behave, think and respond towards the instructions received.

Dimensions of the Human Mind

Basically, the human mind works in six major dimensions. These dimensions are:

Joy

Love

Fear

Boredom

Hatred

Sexuality

It is believed that these dimensions are present in the mind of all human beings. However, their intensity differs from one person to the other. It is actually impossible to eliminate any of these dimensions completely from the mind and those who try to do so only end up suppressing the way their brain performs.

For instance, many people who get misguiding spiritual teachings often try to suppress some dimensions from their mind and this result in some problems that may last for a lifetime. When you seek to understand how the mind operates, you will stop trying to suppress these dimensions and this will give you a better physical and psychological experience in life. Below is a more detailed explanation for each of these dimensions, and how they affect the mind.

1.Love

Love is one of the things that occur naturally in the mind. The human mind expresses this dimension through compassion, tenderness, empathy, charity, romance, service and devotion. Every mind is capable of releasing these expressions in one way or the other. In most cases, the mind triggers this dimension when the person feels secure around the person being loved. The level of love always diminishes when the person feels less secure.

When love occurs at the unconscious level of the mind, it can result in a state of disharmony and imbalance. For instance, when you are obsessed with a person, the mind can lead you into becoming insecure and over-possessive. This can result in over-indulgence in some not-so-good activities that may hurt or drive the one you love away from you. When passion is not controlled by some maturity or wisdom, it can make you a slave to the same thing that you love. This means that for love to work, the conscious mind should be involved.

2.Fear

This is also another nature of the mind. The human mind is, once in a while, controlled by fear. Some people are always more fearful than others. A person who is fearful is always resistant to change, growth and movement. Although this is considered to be a dark nature of the mind, it is impossible to suppress the feeling in the unconscious mind. However, as you become more aware of the feeling and how to control it, you will be able to identify what causes you fear and learn to live with it.

In most cases, when your mind is focused on the cause of fear, you will always have fear-based thoughts. However, when you become more conscious about what is fueling this kind of dimension, your fear will slowly become less intense and you will be able to overcome all your fears.

Fear is one of the several dimensions that awaken the mind. Some forms of fear that are common among people are anxiety, panic, worry, depression, horror, insecurity and nervousness. It is possible to control fear-related thoughts, but it is not possible to get rid of fear in totality. This is because fear is one dimension that is engraved deep in the human mind. The goal of those seeking to overcome fear is always not about getting the mind to stop generating fear, but arriving at an awareness or consciousness that they should not allow their behavior and activities to be influenced by the fear.

3.Boredom

This is another dark nature of the mind. Boredom refers to a state of the mind when you feel disinterested in the present moment. It is one of the most harmless dimensions although when prolonged it may result in depression. In most cases, when boredom occurs you will be triggered to move to more creative activities and environments which can help you develop new interests and desires. When you allow the feeling of boredom to mature, it may result in both mental and physical growth since you will be able to experience new spaces, ideas, and opportunities as you seek to kill the boredom.

Therefore, instead of suppressing the feeling of boredom, allow the mind to process this fully. The result of this will be several inspired actions that will lead you towards joy and fulfillment.

4.Joy

Joy is one of the positive natures of the mind. It refers to the state of being lively and energetic. Most people pursue this dimension because a joyful state makes the body to relax significantly. Some common expressions of joy include calmness, relaxation, enthusiasm, exhilaration, and excitement. Although all minds are able to experience this dimension, some experience it as relaxation while others experience more rigorous feelings like excitement and enthusiasm.

A good number of people always try to suppress this feeling because of other negative feelings existing in their minds like depression and sadness. However, it is advisable that you allow this dimension as much as you can so that you do not end up making some wrong mistakes from suppressing this feeling.

5.Hatred

Hatred is one of the ark natures of the mind. This dimension plays a vital role in identifying your likes and dislikes. Just like any other dimension, you can never get hatred completely out of the mind. Most people who tend to suppress the feeling of hate usually to end up bitter, and with a lot of negative energy. Such energy is highly destructive and toxic.

People express hatred in various ways. These include jealousy, resentment, dislike, stress, anger, impatience, suspicion, criticism, and anger. Once you become conscious of this aspect of the human mind, you will not suppress any feelings of hate. Instead, you will only learn not to personalize any activities and reactions related to this dimension.

When you become conscious about this trait, you will learn to allow the mind to process hate-based thoughts, but you will not waste your time on such. Trying to suppress thoughts that are related to hate only makes them worse since you may start judging yourself based on the negative feeling and it may not be possible to completely take such feelings off your mind.

6.Sexuality

This is a heavy dimension that can be seen either as positive or negative. When handled the wrong way, this dimension may lead to frustration, guilt, and depravity. It also manifests greatly in the physical realm since it involves reproduction. Sexuality also serves as a form of pleasure or entertainment. It is the only dimension that results from other dimensions like joy and love.

Since the energy emanating from this dimension can be so intense, suppressing it often results in disharmony and toxicity in relationships. Individuals who suppress this feeling always end up angry and full of hatred. Sexuality differs among all people. It is affected by several factors including a person's age as well as several dimensions of the mind. For instance, a person whose mind is full of fear often finds it hard to engage in sex. Boredom and hatred can also reduce a person's interest in sex. Love, joy, and peace always translate to a high sex drive. As long as the human mind is healthy and in good operation, it will often depict these six dimensions every day. Mostly, individuals embrace positive natures of the mind like joy and love but tend to ignore the dark natured dimensions such as hatred, boredom, and fear. Being emotionally mature gives you the freedom and ability to express these six dimensions in a way that does not influence others negatively.

Chapter 7 Self-Protection

Know the Strategies

When you know what it takes to brainwash someone, it becomes a lot easier to identify when those strategies are being used on yourself. The more you practice brainwashing others, the easier you are going to be able to identify these unique mannerisms in conversations with other people. This will be important when it comes to protecting yourself against being subjected to mind control. They always say that knowledge is the best prevention, and this is also true when it comes to brainwashing. The more you know, the better.

Don't Buy into Fear

Fear is one of the most popular strategies to manipulate someone into doing whatever you want them to do. It is used by a large majority of the government, media, and general society. This is one of the most popular strategies to get people to do what you want them to do. It has been used to get people to vote for certain government officials, like or dislike certain groups of people, and otherwise behave virtually however someone wants for them to behave.

When you notice scare tactics are being used, take the time to recognize it and do research to know whether or not what is being said holds any validity. This will help you know for sure whether or not you need to agree with the person attempting to brainwash you.

Fear works on the basis that it plays on people's emotions which, as you have learned, is one of the best ways to get people to agree with you. Instead of using logic, you simply use their emotions to get them to do what you want them to do. Make sure that you are not letting others use your emotions against you.

Learn to Consciously Recognize Subliminal Messaging

Subliminal messaging is everywhere in the modern world, and it is important that you do not allow yourself to be subjected to it. Not only is it present in mass media, mass advertising campaigns, and other major messages that are being shared with the world, but it also a part of other areas, too. Even entrepreneurs, independent marketers, and other people are using subliminal messages as an opportunity to get people to do what they want them to do. This is a common strategy that is being used by the average lay person, and it is important that you don't let this strategy be used against you.

Don't Follow the Herd

The herd tends to be guided by the mass media or government, which you have already learned tends to be responsible for brainwashing people. When you follow the herd, you are likely being brainwashed. This works on the basis of having proof: there is a proof that "everyone else is doing it" which might make you feel like you should do it, too. Remember that this is an extremely popular method of mind control, and it can be very easy to be subjected to. We often don't want to be the odd one out or left on the sidelines while everyone else does something, such as buy into trends or believe a certain common belief that may not actually be true to begin with. If you take the time to do research and pay attention to the realistic truth, you will refrain from being brainwashed by anyone else.

Stay in Control of Conversations

Do not let others control conversations with you. When they do, you are more likely to be subjected to brainwashing strategies that will actually have an effect on you. You don't necessarily need to be leading the conversation, but you need to be prepared to actually control the conversation. Part of that may be allowing the other person to believe they are in control when they actually aren't. In doing so, you can actually witness the strategies they are attempting to use and see how they might succeed and where they are failing. This will give you the opportunity to identify where you can do better with your own practice. If you allow others to control conversations and you don't consciously tune into this, you may end up finding that you become subjected to brainwashing strategies by others, which will result in you potentially agreeing to something you don't actually want to agree with.

Trust Your Instinct

When all else fails, trust your instinct. If you practice listening to it, you are more likely to know when someone is trying to brainwash you or get you to think, believe or do things that are not what you actually want to do. Your instinct can almost always identify when someone has ulterior motives and is attempting to get you to do something you don't actually want to. You may get a general feeling that something is wrong, or you may be able to identify exactly where they are trying to manipulate or control you. This will help you prevent yourself from getting brainwashed. You can then either take over the conversation and get into control over the situation, or simply exit the situation altogether.

Reflection

If you find that you have been brainwashed, you should take some time to reflect on the situation. Try and identify what happened that caused for the situation to be effective, and why you were able to be brainwashed. Look for the strategies that were used by the other person and how they were able to work on you. Make sure that you identify the opportunity to use this as a learning curve so that you can prevent yourself from being brainwashed in the future. You should also try and uncover the exact strategies they used so that you can learn a lesson or two from them. After all, if they were able to brainwash you, they must be pretty good at what they do! This means that you will be able to use their techniques going forward to enhance your own abilities and have greater success with mind control going forward.

Once you become a master at mind control yourself, it will be nearly impossible for anyone to use your strategy against you. Really, the only way they can is if they are better than you at your practice. This is why you should aim to become the best. You don't only want to be able to use it to get what you want, but you want to master it to avoid getting what you don't want. The more you practice mastering mind control, the more success you are going to have with it and the less likely you are going to be controlled by anyone else.

Remember, knowledge is the best tool for prevention. If you really want to prevent yourself from becoming brainwashed by anyone else, arm yourself with knowledge of the various methods they could use to brainwash you so that you are less likely to be affected by it.

Additionally, if you find that you ever have been brainwashed, always look at it as an opportunity to learn more about the art. This will give you the chance to master your practice even more, and eventually become the most masterful mind control artist that exists. You will not be able to be brainwashed by anyone once you are fully aware of what it looks like and feels like to be under mind control.

This will also step up your own practice because you will be able to enforce the techniques of others in order to have total success with your own practice.

It is important that you always work towards learning how to prevent yourself from becoming subjected to mind control. You never want your own practice to be used against you, as this will really cripple your confidence and take away from your own success with mind control. Mistakes are bound to happen, but you always want to be aiming higher. Otherwise, you will never be able to have total success in getting your way and having success with mind control because you will be continually under the control of others. This is ineffective and will destroy your success. Do not let this happen.

Chapter 8 All We Have Is A Dark Side

Have you ever thought yourself of creating a negative impact of this life? Sometimes people are engrossed with the right things or morals they have and forget their dark sides. Other scenarios are where one is prized highly even by parents that you value yourself of a higher standard than your counterparts. That feeling is sometimes unfortunate because you may think you are right in anything whereas other individuals see our weakness. That is why it is good to accept all corrections as one cannot identify their ills or wrongs unless you are told.

What about the dark side you have? You may be surprised to know that the dark side in you can be used as an advantage. Sometimes one is too proud to recognize the vices one have. Other people know their vices, and they feel pressured to control them, therefore generating a personality disorder. You may be that guy who is always viewed to be wicked; thus, everybody fears from that character in you. You, therefore, feel isolated and think you cannot do anything to change their perception on you.

Another instance is that you may have been involved in a sorrowful ordeal. Your past tends to determine the life course one chooses. You feel that you cannot try a particular task because you failed once, and you believe you are a complete failure. Maybe at one time, you were short-tempered at an extent of injuring your friend or sibling with a machete. Therefore, you will grow with the attitude that there is a hidden darkness in you.

In some cases, this is the demonic part in you, and you should try to control it in every way. Many relationships have broken because the partners did not take time to know the evil of the other. All they shared is their bright linen, and they did not take time to understand the dirty linen of the other spouse. It would be hurting to know the prince charming or the queen you once believed can hart you in a way you never expected.

Therefore, it is suitable for everybody to recognize the demonic part of you and try to share with anyone who can understand. Moreover, before getting in a relationship, dig at the background to identify the weakness of your beloved. Everybody has the evil spirit inside which you may know or do not. Do you ever think your enemies can ever tell you something positive? But consider asking them of what they hate you for, you may realize they do not hate you but dislikes the vice in you. You may further be surprised that they want you to change for the better. It is essential to know who your real friends are because some are fake friends. They will relate with you to discover your weakness of which they will exploit you negatively.

Having that evil side is sometimes a positive thing because you will know your true nature. Sometimes you are afraid that your close friend will discover your dark side and laugh at you. At other times you like living alone because you feel the demon in you will harm the people you care. Such people experience low self-esteem and do not see any value in themselves. However, there is good news. do you know even the best of you may be the dark side to other people? You may be that bright guy in school or that star player, but do you know too much of anything is poisonous. You are used to being praised or celebrated by your colleagues; therefore you developed that arrogance attitude. Hence that is an evil nature in you.

How Can One Use the Evil Nature in You for Your Advantage?
You use that character one has to know who your real friends are. The worst betrayal is that which comes from close friends. That pal of yours may not even love you but as waiting at that moment you. Sometimes these friends are interested in the possessions or the richness you have, but when poverty strikes you, they will eclipse. Kings or queens are followed because of the influence, wealth, and authority they commission to that kingdom, but not out of the love

the subjects have for them. Your dark nature in you will disconnect you from fake friends and connect you to real allies.

This feeling helps one to have an attitude of self-acceptance. Maybe you have done everything to stop these evils. However, your hustles are fruitless. You eventually feel that it is an epidemic that you cannot fight. However, by realizing your true nature, you will consequently learn that attitude to accept yourself. Therefore, you can face people in confidentially as you feel you have the power to control that evilness you have.

Being weak and feeling disoriented in society is another negative impact of the dark side in you. However, if you learn to manage those feelings, you will have no more fear to face society. You will undoubtedly identify those people who are ready to support you and finish that distrust you possess. Sometimes you may have done wrong that you fear of repeating such actions. Consequently, you even fear yourself, but if you do self-evaluation, you will stop that attitude.

Sometimes the evilness in you can help you to attain you want. You can be dictatorial in any way, but that attitude will command respect and obedient from your subordinates. They will fear you and will try to do everything right to please you. You always have a negative attitude in everything, but you will be a winner if your optimistic friend loses in an area he thought was achievable. If people fear that you will hurt them, they will allow you to do everything that pleases you.

Some scholars say that you can only 'solve evil with evil.' This ideology works when one wants to reduce the vices found in society. You are that saint whom everybody respects, but how can you fight those criminals who fight you if you do not know how they think. Therefore, if you have a Dark side, you will learn about it and recognize how to deal with it. Therefore, if your counterpart has the same element you will be in a position to manage him. That is why most people use reformed addicts or criminals to advise other individuals suffering under the same umbrella.

How Can One Use the Dark Side To Manipulate People?

Many are the cases people are conned, and they often say that the culprit manipulated them. This move can go to an extent where a person is coerced or brainwashed to do something of, not their wish. Manipulation in some people can be viewed as a vice that is not acceptable. It is usually a way of influencing, coercing or persuading a person to agree with what you want. In this case, you are the dominant force, and your counterpart is the less dominant person. Many of the manipulators use different approaches in eliciting you to do what they want. Some may be sweet-talking to influence you to do something that even you did not wish to. Others will forcefully blackmail you or corer you to do a favor,

Manipulation is an example of the dark side that you may possess. Being manipulated sometimes show that you are gullible, and you can easily be fooled to do something that you never wished. Those particular people who influence others are mostly the emotional intelligent guys. Such personnel play around with your feelings and you sense danger you do not follow their instructions. One may ask how the dark nature in you is connected to manipulation. Remember that manipulation may be positive or negative, but in this case, consider manipulation in positive grounds. If you are a parent, you must show you wrong side so that the children can obey you. Imagine how you feared to do wrong when you were a kid because you were afraid of caning from parents. Therefore, the parents will manipulate you in doing something right by using such painful measures. Isn't that the right side of manipulation prompted by the dark side?

What are Yin and Yang

It is a Chinese philosophy that shows how contrary parties or opposite ones may intermingle, connect, and interdepend on each other. You will always feel oriented to mingle with another even if you do not share the same class. This principality is associated with the dark nature one has. Yin is expressed and marked as evil, wicked, feminist, and shadows. While Yang is marked as bright, masculinity, heaven, and eminence, these two groups of people usually relate to energize their colleague. Recognize that Yang is mostly associated with male and Yin is associated with females.

It has been found that both of these qualities very differently and are used in manipulation. A Yin person is characterized by being a listener, softy, coolness, surrender, and respectful. In Yang people, they are portrayed in being brave, authoritative, and strict. Therefore, in most cases, the Yang People Influences the Yin individuals

Chapter 9 Dark Psychology Experts

When we talk about dark psychology, there are people that we encounter every day that are using it and using it on us. You may not consider them to be psychopaths or sociopaths, but when we break down their personality traits, they do possess all of the ones that put them in these categories. Here are a few examples of how they manipulate us in our daily lives.

Narcissists have come up quite a bit in this book so far. We aren't done yet, either! We see and deal with these people every day. They have a huge sense of self-worth and love. They try to get other people to validate them and their beliefs that they are better and more superior to everyone around them. They have dreams of being adored and even worshiped. They do show some dark personality traits and are star manipulators. They can easily persuade others to do anything that they want them to. Their actions are all leading up to how soon they will be worshiped by all who meet them.

Another group of people who are known for using dark psychology is those in politics. Politicians have been put in the realm of dark psychology even before it had a name. Many of them do use tactics that can persuade people to do anything that they want. Look back at Hitler, for example. Politicians want to do one thing: get the votes of the people to take office in a grand home. This is why many of them do use dark psychology.

Sociopaths are another group of people that we have mentioned quite frequently in this book. People that are sociopaths will appear charming to you at first. They will be very intelligent, but they act on their impulses quite a lot. They have problems showing their emotions to people, and they never feel remorse for anything that they do. They use all sorts of shady tactics to persuade people to do what they want them to do. They love to take advantage of people, and we may see these types of people every day in our day-to-day lives. We may even be living with one.

Attorneys are often put in the category of people who are psychopaths. Again, this does not mean that they are killers or crazed. Many of them have specific traits that make them fit into the psychopath category. Some attorneys will focus on a case so much that all they can think of is winning it. They can't imagine what their life is going to be like if they lose this case and they don't care what they have to do to win. Many of them will resort to dark psychology to get the exact thing that they want.

Being in sales is a very tough job that only a few types of people can do. When you are a salesperson, you have to be very focused on making a sale no matter what the customer is telling you. Generally, this could result in the customer feeling that the salesperson was too pushy. Salespeople are generally put in the category of psychopaths because of their focus to make the sale no matter what. Some salespeople will use dark psychology to get the sale even if it does mean lying to the customer.

Leaders are also put into the psychopath category. Not all leaders in the world are bad people, but many in history has shown us differently. We did discuss a few earlier on in this book. Some leaders used their darkest tactics to get what they wanted. They wanted votes, and they wanted their devoted followers to do anything that they were told. Charles Manson and Jim Jones are great examples of leaders who were also psychopaths.

Have you ever heard a public speaker and you were so blown away by what they said? Did you even remember what they said? Public speakers have a way with words, and they will often use shady tactics to reel people in. When they use dark tactics, their words and actions will cause the listeners to have some emotional change when they hear them. This is what makes people believe what the speaker is saying. They move their listeners with emotions and get everyone to buy what they are selling.

The last people on this list are selfish people. We all know them, and they are everywhere in our lives. You could even be one! Selfish people act on what they want, no matter who it hurts along the way. They have an agenda, and it is to take care of no one but themselves. They never meet anyone's needs but their own. This is what causes them to lose friends and loved ones in their lives.

Do you think that you could fit into one of these categories and you're scared to admit it? You can always ask yourself a string of questions to see if you're just paranoid. What is your goal for each interaction that you make? When you meet someone, do you focus on what they can do for you, or do you generally want to get to know them? Do you focus on how they benefit your life? Do you feel good when you leave a new interaction? When you are engaging in a talk with a new person or an old friend, do you feel good about what you are saying or what you are asking of them? Are you honest with them? Do you wonder if they are thinking of using you for benefits that you could give them? Do you ever think of using shady tactics to get more out of them? Think deeply about these questions and how you would answer them. You will soon realize if you do possess the ability to use dark tactics on those around you or if you do not.

Chapter 10 Ways That You Can Predict Other's Minds

You are an expert in beginning psychology now! Since you know all the ways that others might have hurt you, it's now time to take this power and do something good with it. No matter what you might have thought about your brain and your abilities in the past, you understand now that you have so much power that you were just given since birth. These abilities are not easily used. Some people will struggle to ever figure out who they really are and what they want from this life. You might still not know that, and that's perfectly fine. You shouldn't keep yourself perfectly labeled in a box or else this is going to limit your thinking. Whatever others have made you feel in the past does not define who you are now. Learn from your past and don't forget who you are or where you came from. Let go of the hurt you have felt so that you can start healing and moving forward in a more positive direction.

Make sure that you really get to know people. Don't make assumptions. The better that you can really understand a person and who they are at their core, the easier it will be to have a more positive influence over them. Even when you are feeling like you have no idea what you're doing, you can always do some digging internally and externally to discover a greater, more meaningful truth. If you start to make too many assumptions and only allow people to be the labels that you have put on them, this is really going to limit your abilities to grow and understand the world better.

Communication is going to be how it all happens. It is always going to be better to just lay the truth out there and talk it out rather than trying to hold onto things so deeply. Though it might be really scary and challenging, it is going to make you feel so much better in the end when you can speak your truth and let others hear your opinions and feelings. Don't try to persuade in other ways besides communication.

Don't withhold things from people, such as something they might need. You can manipulate others this way, but communication and talking things out is going to be more effective and have longer-term results.

The hurt that you have felt can be used for good now. All you have experienced has led you to right where you are in this moment. The darkest moments that you have gone through that you thought never would end are over now. The times when you wanted to run away and get rid of all of this have brought you to the person that you are now. Though you might never want to go back and do it over again, you should still learn to be grateful for these experiences, because without them, you wouldn't be able to be positively influential person that you are about to become.

Getting to Know Them

Now it is time in the book to start to do the thing that you probably want to more than anything – persuade others! We live in a world where influence is essential. If you can't manage to persuade certain people, then it can keep you back from achieving the things that you really want in this life. The most important thing that you will want to do is get to know who you are trying to persuade. Whether you want to convince your husband that you're ready to have children, or you want to persuade your entire 100-member sales team that they need to push harder to drive sales, it all starts with really getting to know who they are and how they operate.

The first step in this process is to look at their background. How old are they? What gender do they identify as? Where do they live? What are their strengths? What are their weaknesses? What do they have already? What is it that they want? When you can answer these kinds of questions, it will become much easier to know how to come up with a plan of persuasion in order to suit your favor.

Certain kinds of differences will be important in this situation. For example, asking your 18-year-old boyfriend for $20 is going to be done in a different way than you would ask your 80-year-old grandmother for the same thing. In order to persuade people, you have to really understand the things that generically define them and then get into their deeper characteristics, such as things that create the personality that they have.

Next, you will want to determine what their likes are. What things make them happy? These should be easy to understand for people that you already know. When it comes to trying to analyze your customer base if you are trying to persuade sales, then think of basic things they'll like such as discounts, freebies, and other little rewards for being a consumer.

After you have managed to determine what it is that they might like, you should next try and figure out the things that they aren't as big of fans of. This might include things like long return times after purchasing something, having hidden fees, or not being able to customize their products. When you can identify both the things that they like and dislike, then it is easy to act accordingly. For everything that you might have that they will dislike, offer up a solution by providing something that they like. It seems so obvious, but a lot of people who try to influence others will completely disregard this.

Finally, make sure that you are highly aware of the way that they communicate. If you are understanding of this, it will be that much easier to make sure that you are expressing things with them in the same way. Always listen to the other person and ensure that you are giving them a platform to speak. Don't just look at the words they're saying but also their face as they start to share information with you. If someone feels as though they aren't being listened to, it will make them want to turn away from you and they will be far less likely to be persuaded in the end. The subsequent segment is going to discuss further the importance of communication and how you can better enable this kind of healthy interaction in your life.

Understanding the Importance of Communication

Communication isn't easy for everyone. It seems so simple to just open your mouth and start talking. We all do it, sometimes with others, often alone, and sometimes without even thinking before we do start chatting away. It's not uncommon to find that you are struggling to share what you are feeling through the use of your words, even though you are currently experiencing that kind of emotion. The better you are able to communicate, the easier your life is going to be, and the happier you will become in the end.

To start off by bettering your communication skills, remember that it is a practice. There is no pill you can take or secret trick that you can start to do right now. You will have to make sure that you are practicing talking to other people in order to get better at it. If you're just starting, practice first by having small conversations. This might be with a barista at your local coffee shop or someone at the bus stop as you both are waiting. Don't bother other people, of course, but just look for ways that you can articulate your voice and try to say something beyond the basic "how are you?"

Make sure that you are effectively expressing your feelings to yourself. Sometimes when we are all alone, we still won't fully understand what our emotions mean. If you have to, start journaling your feelings every day. The more that you can work them out yourself and write down the emotions that you are feeling, the easier it will be to work through them on your own. How can you expect to effectively share these with others if you aren't sure how to share them with yourself?

When it comes to starting to persuade others, ensure that you are careful with your words. You never want to force anyone to do anything or put them in a place where they might feel as though they have little to know control. Avoid using phrases such as "You should do this." No one wants to be told what to do.

Talk about yourself first. It seems counterintuitive, but people will be more likely to respond by picking up on example rather than having you tell them what to do. For example, let's say that you want to persuade your spouse to start waking up earlier because you think it would help prevent the stress of being late every morning. Rather than saying something such as "You should start to wake up earlier," you can say something such as "I found that by waking up earlier, it's helped me to be a lot less stressed in the morning before work."

Let others believe that the idea is their own. They will want to believe that they were the ones to come up with this plan, not the other way around. Give them the chance to work through the plan on their own, and they can figure out their own positives and negatives. It will be a more effective persuasion when you are able to inspire it within other people rather than forcing them to believe something.

After this, ensure that you are careful of your own tone and body language. Create an atmosphere where they can be comfortable around you. The more calmness, love, and compassion that you can show to them, the easier it will be for them to relate to you. Sometimes we feel as though we need to be rigid and stern in order to get people to do what we want. This isn't the case at all! You should be kind and loving, and others will be much more receptive.

Last but not least, ensure that you are being very respectful of those that you are trying to persuade. You want to make sure that they feel comfortable with you, not as if they need to be ashamed or embarrassed around you. If someone says something stupid, no matter how dumb it sounds, don't make fun of them for it! Don't laugh at people or belittle them for their beliefs. Build others up and you will find that they have that same kind of respect in return.

Chapter 11 The Psychology Of Persuasion

Persuasion is the act of prevailing over another person to believe something by the use of various reasoning or arguments. There is ethical persuasion and dark persuasion. The difference between these two types of persuasions is the intent. An ethical persuader may try to convince another person to do something without giving much thought to certain tactics. They may do this without ulterior motive or real understanding of the person they are trying to persuade. This particular persuader may be concerned with creating good for many people like a diplomat negotiating against the war. This is the persuader known to be ethical.

On the other hand, there is a dark persuader. This particular individual is well aware of the bigger picture. He has a full understanding of the person he is trying to persuade, what motivates them, and to what extent they can go for their tactic to be successful. A dark persuader is not concerned with how moral their manipulation is doing the right thing is not their motivation. When a dark persuader identifies a thing they want, they devise a way to get it and do not care who gets hurt in the process. Their goal is to always get what benefits them no matter the cost.

When is Persuasion used?

Persuasion is used every day by every person in various ways. Children use persuasion to get their parents to do for them what they want or buy for them something. In intimate relationships, partners persuade each other in order to get what each wants. Persuasion in business is common. A business owner needs to persuade his or her customers to buy their services or products. Persuasion is common and can be ethical or unethical depending on the intent of the person doing the persuasion.

Different techniques are used to persuade individuals. These techniques can be used for both dark persuasion and ethical persuasion. The outcome of any form of persuasion is to get your opponent, partner or audience to do as you wish them to do so that you benefit. It becomes unethical persuasion when the only person that stands to gain is the one doing the persuasion. When it is only one person gaining, it means it is getting what a person wants at the expense of the other person.

Persuasive techniques used

Persuasion is used to convince a person about something they would not have considered otherwise. Advertisements are one-way persuasion techniques are employed. The same techniques used to sell a good thing can be used to manipulate a person. There are other ways a person can persuade you, these include:

Appealing to authority – if you are trying to persuade a person into doing something, using important people or experts to pass your point across is very convincing. When you reliably research, you can make your argument very convincing and sway your audience. For instance, a person can say:

Example - The former first lady Michele Obama has said the only way to eradicate obesity among children is getting rid of junk food from vending machines.

Example – according to a recent study, watching TV reduces stress causing a reduction in the risk of heart diseases.

Both these statements whether true or falsified can convince a person that what is being said is true because a person has appealed to authority. Dark persuasion can also appeal to authority in order to convince their victim to do as they wish for them to do.

Appeal to reason – people are easily convinced when a person uses logic to persuade them. For instance, a person would say:

A bar of chocolate contains 300 calories and 20 grams of sugar. That is not so bad! You can still enjoy you're a bar of chocolate every day because it is within your caloric limit.

Although that statement is not entirely true, a person that wants you to push their sales, yet they know it is not healthy for you will use it to persuade you. People tend to trust where there are figures believing the information to be authentic. This tactic is widely used to manipulate individuals to do as other wishes.

Empathize or appeal to emotion – making a person feel sad, angry or happy can help you persuade them. For instance:

A person may say to you that your donation is important because it may feed a hungry child for a day or

If you do not donate, a child will go hungry and die and you will be part of the reason.

Both those statements serve to persuade an individual to make a contribution. The first one appeals to the person to empathize with a situation while the second statement serves to guilt-trip the individual. Both statements are aimed at getting a contribution. However, one is used in an ethical way while the other is unethical or dark persuasion.

Appealing to Trust – if a person trusts and believes you, it becomes easier to persuade them. Most psychopaths make sure their victims trust them and that is how they are able to persuade them. It is almost impossible to persuade a person that doesn't trust you. Trust is important if one is to be convinced. For instance:

If a person seems to be doing well financially and tells you to invest in something, they may say to trust them that are how they began. They know you are desperate to have financial stability and because you may know their story, you will believe them.

If this person is genuine, then you are likely to have made a good investment. However, embezzlers, on the other hand, are people that are also trusted by those that invest with them. They convince their victims to invest in a certain thing because it pays. You trust them because they seem to have a good reputation and seem to know what they are doing. Unfortunately, this person is appealing to your trust to invest your hard-earned money, but they swindle you. This is dark persuasion in play. All the people that have had their funds embezzled trusted their embezzlers.

Plain folk – manipulators know to persuade their victims or audience; they must appear to be the average kind of a person. For instance, politicians use persuasion tactics to get voters. He or she may just say:

"I am an average person. I relate to the suffering we have endured under the current leadership and it is time we changed the narrative. I have grown up with you in this neighborhood, I have faced the same challenges and therefore I am the best candidate."

This kind of appeal is to show that a politician is an average person just like the voters. The politician wants the voters to believe he can relate with them because he is one of the – ordinary. Whether the information is true or not, whether the politician just wants votes and will do nothing or not, he will manage to convince the electorate through such statements.

Bandwagon – this is the presumption that everyone trusts it, so it must be good or true. This is very common in advertisements. For instance:

A company advertising its brand of toothpaste may claim that 2 out of every American household use this product. It has been trusted by families for generations to offer the best in cavity protection.

No one wants to have cavities. If you are convinced that that product is the number one bestseller and the majority of the people trust it, you will definitely buy it. It is important to remember that some of these statistics are not true. To push sales of a product regardless of if the product does perform as indicated, companies can come up with untruths.

Bandwagon is also a tactic used majorly on social media. If a person notices many likes regarding a particular product, they rush out to buy it. The assumption is that if many like it, it must be good. However, it is possible that it is the advertisement that was well crafted and not the product.

Rhetorical Question – when a person wants to persuade another one, they will use rhetorical questions. For instance, if a person is promoting a skin care regiment, they may ask their audience, "Who wouldn't like to have fair glowing skin?" the answer is obvious. It provokes the person to think and wish to have flawless skin and end up buying the product.

Another person may want to sell you shares knowing very well that the share value is likely to drop. They show you convincing figures and ask you, "wouldn't you want to make money?" Even the richest person in the world wants to make more money! This kind of tactic will end up convincing you to invest even though it could be a wrong investment.

Chapter 12 What Is Manipulation

When coming from a psychological point of reference, manipulation is mostly about perception. How we perceive things or actions determines our laws, social formalities, and even our lives.

The manipulator changes these norms with tactics. The determination of the positive or negative connotation of these actions remains subjective. Psychological manipulation is often considered devious. With the subject of dark psychology, we can take into account that the manipulation practiced is often exploitative at the expense of others.

So, what is manipulation of the dark?

Sources tell us that it is concealment—hiding in the shadows knowing when to strike. It is also a false front, hiding true intentions. When we are talking about this level of deception, we are talking about hiding aggression. When we take, there is a certain level of aggressive behavior that happens. A small part of manipulation is hiding that aggressive behavior so that the victim sees only good nature.

This is accomplished by various ways and means, one being knowledge. When we allow another to know us, we display vulnerability along with strengths. The knowledge of these personal traits can give the manipulator the ability to maneuver around without any alarms going off.

The effectiveness of manipulating those strengths and vulnerabilities arrives when the practitioner of the dark knows what is vulnerable and what inspires pride.

A reoccurring ideology that drives us to war takes into consideration that war is more negative than positive. We want to avoid it. The manipulation process sees the pride in all of us and plays to that pride. It is our strength. However, when used to drive an army to slaughter others, intention of our pride has been manipulated to enforce the agendas of others.

There is ruthlessness when we talk about psychological manipulation. When dealing with someone other than the pure psychopath who feels little to nothing, ruthlessness can be measured. Often soft ruthless behavior can sneak up on its prey and snag it before it knows what is happening. This harm of the prey becomes less than even a momentary qualm in the mind of the manipulator.

Often the practitioners of dark psychology use aggression and fear to drive us. The less dark side still falls into the category of knowing what weakness is, and that weakness leaves the individual open to control.

How the manipulator uses that control determines the severity of manipulation. There is and are positive versions of manipulating others. Like convincing someone that they are not doing well and that they need to get help. We, however, are looking at the darker side of this. The manipulator uses their skills of control to get what they want—and the cost does not apply.

There are many ways to move another into a place of being controlled. From the positive to the negative, psychological manipulators utilize all tactics.

When positive reinforcement is used, charm is displayed. A forced smile or laughter can trigger laughter in all of us. As when we were infants, we copy what we see. When we see tears, we want them to stop. When we see a smile, we find ourselves smiling as well.

The manipulator using positive reinforcement can shower money, charm and gifts to get us to feel something. The usage of these things allows control of us on an instinctual level. We follow those who tell us what we want to hear.

Psychological manipulation can also implement negative reinforcement. This is a form of deflection. A substitution of one thing for another

Often, we have things we need or have to do and we do not really want to do them. The psychological manipulation of negative reinforcement uses that power of negativity to lure the subject from their original need, pushing them toward something they want done instead. The long game, a slow play of putting tasks into another's life and then controlling those tasks so that the manipulator can get what they want is an extremely effective and subdued tactic.

Sometimes only partial reinforcement is required to gain control. We are talking about elevating the fear or doubt regarding the tasks needed done. The partial is the long play. It knows that in the end, the victim will lose. It knows that by planting small seeds now, victory will eventually happen. It knows that we all have our weaknesses and that by planting even a small seed we can take someone to that weakness. An individual trying to work toward something they already were shaky on, or had doubts about, will listen to the lie and flow with that idea, and use it to their own destruction.

The partial manipulator only needs to put the thought in the mind, knowing the weakness is already there, and utilizing it will take their prey to a destructive end.

Psychological manipulators flat, outright punish. From an actual physical lashing to the passive aggressive playing of the victim, punishment is very effective when one wants to control another.

We skulk and cry and yell and nag and go completely silent. This is the blackmail of the manipulator. It inspires guilt in us. That "wanting to be the better person" rises to the front and we do what the manipulator wants.

When the manipulator sets free the crocodile tears, we have no idea if they are real or not. The degree of crying is not up to us to determine. Only the manipulator knows if the tears are legitimate or not.

In this case, the trap is often sprung from the victim side. They walk up to the hurt individual to help, only to find that the manipulator is just lying in wait to strike.

One extreme version of manipulation is violence.

Violence triggers something inside us. We often do anything to avoid it. The manipulator knows that violence strategically applied can make us go into a state of avoidance. There incites the control. Physical violence can have mental scarring. The manipulator causes the scarring. It places violence in tactical places to get the result they want.

Some would say this is the darkest of the dark.

Taken to the individual, this can mentally damage them for a long period of time, if not permanently. Placed on a world stage, it can lead all the way up to the physical conflict of genocide.

The manipulation process in dark psychology is normally not a single move. It is a complex series of moves, often with the outcome only known by the manipulator. The motivations of manipulators are as convoluted as human nature.

Mostly it is about gain. Manipulators of the dark want to gain... something. When we speak about gain, we are talking about power and influence, control and manipulation over others. The trophy is up to the individual. This can be everything as to gaining affections, to money, and even to life itself.

It is about gaining for their personal reasons and gratifications. The taking of others and making the power and control their own Selfishness to the extreme. The mind of the dark practitioner sees the ultimate win as gain over others.

They have power. Superiority is the power over another and taking of someone else's power makes them feel superior. This is a huge driving force behind the manipulator. Often, in the case of immature individuals driving manipulations toward superiority, any is pushed aside for just the feeling of being superior.

In relationships, it is about control. The manipulation of power can put one in control. Although we have looked at the role of the vampire and power, and we know who really has control.

This feeling of control can be overwhelming to the mental state of the dark. Almost drug-like, it is a feeling of emotion that is most logical. Control is one of the easiest manipulation tactics to achieve with only logic to guide. It drives not only the victim, but the manipulator as well.

Psychological manipulation can also be about self-esteem. The self of the manipulator is always in question. This is one of the reasons they manipulate, to define themselves. How easily they are able to manipulate another can tell the dark that they are better than others. That weakness and strength can be measured in the tactical playing field of the hustle.

This defines who they are. Can they manipulate? Yes? They are stronger. No? They are weaker. It is a measuring device for self-esteem.

However, we are not saying it is the only device for measurement. Self-esteem can be measured by far fewer damaging means.

The mind gets bored. And what do we do when we get bored? We seek entertainment. How do we achieve entertainment? We manipulate.

We all do it.

Let us assume we are bored, and we want to remove or alleviate that boredom with something else. Do we just sit back and wait for something new to happen?

No. We actively search for something to replace boredom. Manipulation can take place on many different levels, as well as the severity of which they are applied. From picking up a crayon and coloring, to taking a mental absence, to massacring everyone around you.

The dark psychological manipulator is bored most of the time. More than most the psychological manipulator will often use manipulation to determine their own validity of feelings and emotions

What this boils down to is that manipulation applied in relations with others helps the manipulator to regulate reactions to validate or not validate their own emotions. The manipulator measures the self and their self-esteem by how others handle their personal self-questioning.

This happens when the practitioner does not have a grasp on what emotions are. They look at their own emotions as invalid and manipulate the situation in such a way as to validate them.

We are stuck with ourselves, and we cannot get away. Psychological manipulators validate or invalidate themselves by the tactical controlling of others. It is an interesting way of viewing life, although there is one form of manipulation that we all idolize.

The con

One common form of manipulation is the convincing of another to make their money yours.

This is a hidden agenda of the criminal. This form of mental manipulation preys mostly on the elderly and the rich. However, we all can fall to this form of manipulation. What we choose to spend on and what we do not is our response to a form of psychological manipulation.

Something happens when the buck is passed over. We go from manipulation into action. Something drives us. It is within us and it is outside forces that drive. What causes this drive and the drive itself is called...?

Persuasion

Chapter 13 When And Why To Use Manipulation

Who Manipulates?

Manipulators come in several forms. Some are younger and simply have not learned how to interact with the world. Others still just happen to be manipulative by nature—they are intentionally using their abilities to get what they want with no regard for how it hurts other people. Ultimately, however, the manipulators tend to have several traits in common.

They are always the victim

It does not matter what has happened—the manipulator will always be the victim or not at fault in some way. The manipulator could pull out a gun and shoot you and would rationalize that he had no choice and insist that he was the victim as he holds the smoking gun in his hand. This is a common trait of manipulators as it makes them deserving of sympathy, which gives them the upper hand in many different situations. They will try to figure out how to get all of your friends and family on their side and will blame everything on you. The worst part is that since they are so skillful at doing exactly this, they can often convince other people to fall for it.

They regularly distort the truth

The manipulator will always twist reality. Skilled at weaving webs of lies, the manipulator will always have a way to rewrite history, change a situation, or otherwise make it, so their narrative is the correct one.

They are passive-aggressive

Manipulators tend to be passive-aggressive. A part of this is to make sure that you know your place around the manipulator—they use it to assert dominance and covertly exert their own influence and desire over you. For example, they will intentionally use passive-aggression to make you feel bad, and then be satisfied that they held power necessary to make you feel bad in the first place.

They will pressure you

The manipulator is convinced that he is always right no matter what, and with that in mind, he will not hesitate to pressure you in order to get whatever he wants from you at any given moment. He knows that his way is the right way, and he will force the point until you agree.

They will not work to solve a problem

If you find that there is a problem with the manipulator, good luck—they will not work to come to some sort of solution. Instead, they will continue on as if nothing is wrong, or at the very least, that nothing is wrong with them. They could not care more about your own problems, so long as they are not the manipulator's problems.

They will always keep the advantage

The manipulator has an uncanny way to always remain in control in nearly any situation. They will oftentimes find a way to ensure that they can find a way to stay in charge. They will always pick the restaurant that you go to, or they will always invite you out of your comfort zone and into theirs, all done intentionally to maintain power and control over the situation. When they do this, they effectively guarantee that they are able to stay in charge long enough to keep you off balance and make sure that they always have the upper hand.

They will always have excuses

When they do happen to make a mistake, manipulators typically will have some sort of excuse. There was a car accident on the way over, or they just got fired for no reason at all. It does not matter what the problem is; there will be some sort of excuse that will arise to take the blame away from the manipulator and push it onto someone else.

They will make you feel unconfident

Something about the manipulator will always leave you feeling incompetent and unable to do anything right. This means that you will constantly be feeling like you are the problem rather than seeing that the whole problem may have been resting firmly with the manipulator all along.

Why Manipulate?

Manipulators have all sorts of reasons to manipulate others, with some simply having no reason at all. When you begin to understand the motivation behind these drives, you may be more inclined to understand those techniques that the manipulators everywhere tend to use. This means then that you will be able to figure out how to fight back. You can defend yourself and others based on the knowledge that you have. Knowing why people manipulate others can be a critical skill to develop if you want to be successful in the world around you.

They want to advance in life

When you feel like you need to advance somehow, whether due to needing the money in order to get what you wanted or needed, manipulation is one way to get it. When you manipulate someone, you are usually using them as a sort of steppingstone for yourself in order to ensure that you can, in fact, withstand future struggles while also progressing agenda that you have. Typically, this is the most selfish of the reasons on this list—these manipulators do so simply because they can.

They need power and superiority

Similar to the last reason for manipulation, oftentimes, manipulators need to feel like they are in power. They simply are only secure in themselves so long as they are in a position of power over other people. If they feel like their superiority will be questioned in any way, shape, or form, they will feel insecure. They will feel like the only way they can make themselves feel comfortable is if they exert and enforce their own superiority, which they give themselves through making a point to manipulate those around them.

They need control

When people are particularly controlling, they may find that manipulation is one of the easiest ways to get the results desired. When you are able to manipulate someone else into doing what they need to do, you are able to ensure that you maintain control in nearly any situation. You may have to find a way to covertly encourage the other person to do what you want, but as soon as you manage to do that, you can effectively maintain control, even if the other person does not realize that you are in control of the situation at hand. The need to be in control can be particularly motivating for people when it comes to deciding to manipulate.

They need to manipulate to better their own self-esteem

Some people, such as narcissists, tend to feel like they are only comfortable with themselves when other people are lavishing them with attention or admiration. These people tend to result in manipulation to get that attention, especially if they are not particularly outstanding or deserving of attention in the first place. In manipulating other people into giving them the craved attention, they are able to feel better about themselves.

They are bored

Some people simply enjoy watching the world burn and will make it a point to manipulate other people simply to get entertainment. They treat it like a game or a challenge, intentionally testing boundaries to see how far they can get with no real reason or motivation beyond being bored to guide them. These may be some of the more dangerous manipulators as they have no real goal in mind—they simply want to wreak havoc and spend some time messing with other people despite not getting anything other than their own satisfaction in return.

They have a hidden agenda

More often than not, the manipulator has some sort of reason to manipulate those around him or her. This is typically hidden from the target but can be figured out with enough time and information. Think about how some people will intentionally seek out vulnerable people with ulterior motives. They may marry in order to get their hands-on money, or intentionally volunteer as a caregiver for an elderly family member in order to steal money from them. No matter what the hidden agenda is, the manipulator has good cause to try to keep it hidden.

They do not properly identify with the emotions of others

Sometimes, the manipulation is unintentional and a side effect of simply being unable to identify with other people. Effectively, they lack empathy, and that lack of empathy is enough to make it so they cannot easily identify when they have done something that is manipulative, nor do they automatically recognize when what they have done is problematic. These are people who simply do not understand social norms for some reason or another. They may have a personality or other mental health disorder.

When Manipulation Occurs

No one wants to be on the receiving end of manipulation, and yet it seems to be all around us. The world is literally surrounded by different people and their attempts to manipulate. You can see it on television and in the media. You can see it in religion and politics. It happens in all kinds of relationships when they become unhealthy. There is no real way to truly avoid manipulation and that in and of it can be incredibly disheartening.

However, because manipulation is everywhere, it becomes prudent to understand what it looks like in a wide variety of situations and cases. You want to be able to notice when it is happening and figure out how best to fight back from it to ensure that you actually are able to protect yourself. When you are able to protect yourself from manipulation, you can guarantee that you, at the very least, are not regularly being used by other people simply because you refuse to allow yourself to be

We will take a look at manipulation in several different relationships and contexts for a brief overview of what to expect and why it happens.

In relationships

This is particularly referring to romantic relationships. Romantic relationships seem to attract manipulation frequently, especially if one member of the couple happens to be on the less confrontational side and is afraid of ever standing up for him or herself. When this happens, you may find that you have run into quite the conundrum—you need to figure out how best to leave a romantic relationship rife with manipulation, which can be difficult if the manipulator has done his job right.

In friendships

Manipulative friends may try to get on your good side as quickly as possible, but they will soon fall into the habit of always needing you but never being available when you need them. At first, you will assume it is a coincidence, but over time, you will realize that it is actually a pattern, leaving you stuck to decide whether you would like to leave the friendship altogether or if you would prefer to instead put up with the manipulator's lack of support and enjoy what you can.

In churches

Churches commonly also manipulate people, attempting to force them into situations and actions that they may not necessarily want. In particular, you will commonly see threats of damnation and punishment if they do not live by a very specific life, and that is a perfect example of manipulation. They use their authority to sort of force your hand and make you feel like you have no choice but to comply. This is what they count on—they assume that you will continue to donate, to serve, and to attend because they threaten you if you do not. While many people may not see it as a threat, being told that you may be excommunicated or that you will be damned for eternity are two ways to sort of scare someone into behaving a certain way.

Chapter 14 The Pillars Of Manipulation

1. They use storytelling

Being able to tie stories into logical facts is a brilliant tactic attorney use because the brain is more likely to enjoy listening to a story and absorb the point being made, more than it will when being inundated with a barrage of facts and statistics.

Stories will often bypass the logical part of the brain and make one think more with their emotions than facts will, and this is what you want when trying to establish a strong case for yourself.

Just be careful of someone trying to use this tactic against you and making you fall for a bad argument due to them drawing your logical mind into the nearly hypnotized state that comes with being absorbed by a good story. It increases your suggestibility and reduces your ability to focus on the facts.

2. They know their audience

Great attorneys make it a point to do background checks on the potential jurors and judges they may have to deal with and try their hardest to make sure they can control who is selected to sit in on their cases. If they can control that element, they try to make their arguments, cases, and general way of communicating suit the audience they will be presenting to.

You never know when you might find yourself in a situation when you have to communicate effectively with people who are not used to your usual style. It is imperative that you know as much as you can about the people you speak to if you are to sway them to come over to your side.

You want to learn to communicate with them on their level and avoid the risk of not getting what you want due to minor miscommunications and misunderstandings.

3. They show and not tell where possible

The mind is more drawn in by stories and pictures than it is by pure facts alone. They are often more interesting and easier for the brain to absorb than dates, studies, and statistics. The best attorneys know this better than anyone and use it to their full advantage. They will present evidence where possible, instead of simply referring to it. They will keep referring back to it, even though the audience knows it's there, to keep reinforcing the 'truthfulness' of their cases and re-establishing themselves as the authority in that specific encounter as they have visual evidence of irrefutable truth.

Be aware of someone who constantly harping on about a piece of evidence they may have shown you. Question it despite seeing it. Make sure that you are not falling for the old trick of misdirection just to be misled by a nefarious manipulator.

4. They are reasonable

There are moments when digging in your heels and locking your jaw can play against you even when you are in the right. Great attorneys know this and can recalibrate themselves to suit the interaction and better increase the chances of them getting what they want.

You can consider doing this in your own life where you find small points where you agree with your opponent to lower their defenses. Once their guard is down, you can go back and show them the logic in your own point of view.

This can be a great tactic since people are more likely to dig their heels in when it seems force is the only way out, so suddenly changing the game on them can confuse them into thinking they are getting what they want (to be understood by others) while you are secretly just ensnaring them in your trap from a different angle.

5. They appeal to emotion

There is nothing stronger than being able to use emotions to keep someone off balance and have them eating out of the palm of your hand. Attorneys will often do this by making witnesses angry on the stand to make them slip up in their testimony, if it suits them; making a jury feel bad for a defendant whether or not they are guilty; making potential clients trust them, whether it's in the best interest of the client or not.

Make sure to always keep your head and use your opponent's emotions against them where possible. Winning or losing at games of manipulations often comes down to emotions more than they do with facts. Whether you are trying to convince or prevent yourself from being convinced, keeping your emotions in check while making sure your target does not will be the deciding factor in you walking away as the victim or victor in these kinds of insidious games.

6. They watch the audience's body language

Body language is often a huge deciding factor in how people see you and how they communicate as well. You will often see the best attorneys change their swagger according to the situation so that their message is being communicated on multiple levels. Moreover, body language taps into people's' mirror neurons and can have their instinct to imitate be used against them.

Mirroring someone's body language can make them feel accepted or slightly intimidated, as if you are reading their minds. Seeing someone mirroring you is often a sign that they are more likely to believe what you are saying. At other times, you want to use this to see how people feel about you and react accordingly where necessary.

Body language skills can be a tool for reading minds and controlling emotions.

7. They use leading questions

Leading questions is the favorite technique of many people in the legal business because it allows them to control perspectives, which can win or lose cases and future clients.

If someone asks you, "how much do you hate hockey?" They are not giving you the option of liking hockey. The question already assumes you agree with the person asking it and simply demands the degree to which you agree to show that you are on their side.

Be careful of people using questions like this against you. This tactic can have you not realizing that you are being lured into the trap of accepting a premise that is not true to you. Persuasion is not about right or wrong, it's about winning.

8. They make sure to stay the course of their arguments

You won't often see expert attorneys getting side-tracked trying to defend non-arguments or even their own dignity unless the case depends on it. The best of them will always make it a point to stay the course of their argument while trying to trip up their opposition with the details of their own arguments.

This is a crucial lesson to learn if you want to be more convincing in your own life. You want to be able to make your own statements and arguments seem stable and concrete while subtly destabilizing that of your opponent. You want them abandoning their game to play yours. Once you have them playing your game, you have secured victory. All you need to do is keep them in your world.

9. Taking the advisor role

The best salespeople never come across as though they are trying to sell you something right out the gate. They approach as though they are your advisor, guiding you to finding the best product for you.

10. Listening skills

The best salespeople know how to listen closely for the smallest detail that might help them close the deal. It might be a sign of hesitation, confidence anything that tells them if you are a target, they should be spending their time on and how they should know if it is time to move on.

Usually, we end up being the ones to give these salespeople all the information they need to handle us better. All they usually have to do is listen as we over-answer simple questions and give ourselves away.

11. Empathy

A salesperson who can get under the skin of a prospective client is often more likely to have higher sales because they are able to build a far better rapport with the people they interact with and make them feel safe and secure.

12. Assuming the sale

Salespeople these days no longer ask you if you want to buy their product or not. More often than not they will ask for your details and ask you to sign on the dotted line as if you already agreed to make the purchase.

This often tricks a lot of people into buying things since they don't realize they are being baited into buying something until they're already signing. This tactic is also useful because it takes the choice away from the buyer and puts it in the salesperson's hands.

13. Confidence

People are a lot more likely to buy with their feelings than with their heads, so a confident salesperson can be highly effective because people are more likely to want to trust them simply because of their confident demeanor.

It's natural to want to follow the lead of someone when they seem like they know exactly where they are going. Salespeople use this information to the fullest by starting the sale with a confident body language that engages you even before any words have been spoken.

14. Creating a scarcity mindset

The best salespeople know that scarcity and novelty often play a huge role in how we put a value on things. They use this information to make their product seem more valuable by making customers think that this is the best deal they will ever get. They further reinforce this by making customers think that the offer will only stand for a limited time because this is the last one, or another customer showed interest in buying it as well.

Always take your time to know when this pressure is being applied to you or how you could apply it on an unsuspecting victim.

15. Honesty (where possible)

One of many tactics' salespeople have in common with attorneys is their ability to manipulate the truth. They know how to omit certain truths or simply bend the truth where possible to ensure you see the picture the way they want you to.

They will tell the truth where possible and avoid it where necessary. As long as it benefits them, they will play with the truth as much as possible while maintaining a sense of plausible deniability. This way they can practice deception without lying. They escape on a technicality.

Chapter 15 Difference Between Persuasion And Manipulation

Calling somebody manipulative is an analysis of that individual's character. Saying that you have been controlled is an objection about having been dealt with severely. Control is dodgy, best-case scenario, and out and out corrupt at the very least. In any case, why would that be? What's going on with control? Individuals impact each other constantly, and in a wide range of ways. In any case, what separates control from different impacts, and what makes it unethical? The contrast among influence and control has been a subject of discussion for truly a great many years. In old Greece, during the fourth century BC, the dad of influence, Aristotle, contradicted a gathering of educators known as the Sophists. The Sophists gave guidance in different orders but became infamous for their educating of talk. Aristotle conflicted with the Sophists over the way that they couldn't have cared less about truth yet would advance any thought for a charge. Aristotle attested that the Sophists were participating in control since they intentionally deceived people and caused harm.

Today, the discussion among influence and control seethes on. Many admit that they make some hard memories recognizing the two. However, understanding the differentiation is crucial in light of the fact that it will direct you in affecting others morally and furnish you with the information to perceive manipulative messages.

We are continually liable to endeavours at control. Here are only a couple of models. There is 'gas lighting,' which includes urging somebody to question her very own judgment and to depend on the controller's recommendation. Remorseful fits make somebody feel unreasonably regretful about neglecting to do what the controller needs her to do.

Appeal offensives and friend pressure instigate somebody to think such a great amount about the controller's endorsement that she will do as the controller wishes.

They are publicizing controls when it urges the crowd to shape false convictions, as when we are advised to accept that singed chicken is a health food, or broken relationship, as when Marlboro cigarettes are attached to the tough life of the Marlboro Man. Phishing and different tricks control their victims through a mix of duplicity (from inside and out deceives caricature telephone numbers or URLs) and playing on feelings, for example, greed, fear, or sympathy. At that point, there is increasingly direct control, maybe the most celebrated case of which is when Imago controls Othello to make doubt about Desdemona's loyalty, playing on his insecurities to make him jealous and working him up into a fury that leads Othello to kill his love. Every one of these instances of control shares a sense of immortality. Would it be that they share for all intents and purposes?

Maybe control isn't right since it hurts the individual being controlled. Surely, control frequently hurts. If effective, manipulative cigarette promotions add to malady and demise, manipulative phishing and different tricks encourage data fraud and different types of misrepresentation; manipulative social strategies can support oppressive or undesirable connections; political control can instigate division and debilitate majority rules system. However, control isn't constantly destructive.

Assume that Amy left an abusive-yet-faithful partner; however, in a moment of weakness, she is enticed to return to him. Presently imagine that Amy's companions utilize similar procedures that Imago utilized on Othello. They control Amy into (erroneously) accepting and being offended that her ex-partner was oppressive, yet unfaithful also. If this manipulation prevents Amy from accommodating, she may be in an ideal situation than she would have been had her companions not controlled her. However, too many, it could at present appear to be ethically dodgy.

Naturally, it would have been ethically better for her companions to utilize non-manipulative intends to help Amy abstain from falling away from the faith. Something remains ethically questionable about control, in any event when it helps as opposed to hurts the individual being controlled. So, hurt can't be the explanation that control isn't right.

Maybe manipulation isn't right since it includes procedures that are characteristically unethical approaches to treat other individuals. This idea may be particularly speaking to those propelled by Immanuel Kant's thought that high quality expects us to regard each other as rational beings as opposed to unimportant items. Maybe the main legitimate approach to impact the behaviour of other sound creatures is by discerning influence, and subsequently, any type of impact other than balanced influence is ethically inappropriate. In any case, for all its appeal, this answer also misses the mark, for it would denounce numerous types of impact that are ethically kind.

For instance, quite a bit of Imago's control includes engaging Othello's feelings. Be that as it may, enthusiastic interests are not constantly manipulative. Moral influence regularly offers to sympathy, or endeavours to pass on how it would feel to have others doing to you what you are doing to them. Additionally, getting somebody to fear something that truly is dangerous, to feel guilty about something that truly is shameless, or to feel a sensible degree of trust in one's real capacities, don't appear control. Indeed, even invitations to question one's judgment probably won't be manipulative in circumstances where, maybe because of intoxication or strong emotions, there truly is a valid justification to do as such. Only one out of every odd type of non-sound impact is by all accounts manipulative.

Persuasion is tied in with introducing the entirety of the correct contentions in the most legitimate and persuading way. Control also suggests bending reality to meet the last objective.

In spite of the fact that persuasion additionally suggests convincing an individual to accomplish something they would not at first like to do, it is the transparency and the great expectation behind it that make it socially worthy. An individual can persuade a constructor who needed to drive an undertaking aside to begin it sooner since they have to move into the house by a specific date. The arguments exhibited are genuine, and the goal is transparent. Controlling the constructor would mean saying that the spouse is pregnant and going to conceive an offspring at any minute, even though there is no wife included. This is the reason there is also a social disgrace on control. This is common because of the way that individuals feel like they have been misled and constrained into tolerating something.

Another great difference between the two lies in the way that the individual who has been convinced to receive an alternate sentiment is persuaded. This is the ideal approach. They have been given the entirety of the contentions and are equipped with what they have to put forth a defense for their new choice whenever. At the point when control is included, there is moment lament in the wake of having concurred. This is because no genuine contentions have been utilized; there is no verification of good purpose, and the controller profits by everything more.

- **Why Persuasion Is Good**

To precisely perceive the contrast between persuasion and control, it is basic to comprehend the morals that undergird persuasion. There are some correspondence scholars who have announced that influence is "morally neutral." That is to state that influence is neither great nor awful, yet simply a fair procedure. In any case, I don't acknowledge this position. I would fight that the Aristotelian perspective that influence isn't nonpartisan, yet honourable, is right. Aristotle focused on that influence is characteristically great since it is one of the essential methods through which truth becomes known. Through the enticing strategy, thought is advanced with proof, and an individual is permitted to freely decide to either acknowledge or dismiss that persuasive appeal. Jay Conger expounded on this when he confirmed, "Influence does undoubtedly include moving individuals to a position they don't presently hold, however not by asking or wheedling. Rather, it includes careful preparation, the best possible framing of contentions, the introduction of striking supporting proof, and the push to locate the right enthusiastic match with your audience."

The belief that persuasion is a fair and powerful method for landing at truth is seen by the way that it is the reason for current financial matters, guiding practices, and the lawful framework Furthermore, influence is additionally the establishment of majority rule government. As Professor Raymond Ross states, "Vote based systems utilize thoughtful, ethical persuasion at whatever point they choose pioneers, build up laws, or attempt to ensure their citizens." Even the individuals who become overwhelmed with the idea of persuasion can't escape it. Persuasion is imbued inside human correspondence. When conveying, individuals both purposefully and unexpectedly advance certain convictions and practices. Subsequently, persuasion doesn't involve decisions; it is inherent in the social association. It is so pervasive in human correspondence that, on occasion, it turns out to be practically imperceptible. Dr. Herbert W. Simons, Professor at Temple University, delineates this when he expresses, "The so-called people callings, legislative issues, law, social work, directing, business the board, promoting, deals, advertising, the service, should be called influence professions."

At its center, persuasion is the quest for truth. It is through persuasion that positive change happens. For instance, convincing messages have been deductively demonstrated to invite secondary school students to refrain from smoking, increment lifesaving blood donations, and keep youth from joining gangs. Persuasion Communication researchers Gass and Seiter echo this thought when they attest, "Influence helps produce harmony understandings between countries. Persuasion assists open with increasing shut social orders. Persuasion is vital to the fund-raising efforts of charities and philanthropic organizations. Persuasion persuades drivers to lock in when driving or to avoid driving when they've had a couple of such a large number of beverages. Persuasion is utilized to persuade a drunkard or medication subordinate relative to look for proficient assistance. Persuasion is how the mentor of a dark horse group moves the players to give it their everything Persuasion is an apparatus utilized by guardians to ask kids not to acknowledge rides from outsiders or to enable anybody to contact them such that feels awkward. So, persuasion is the foundation of various positive, prosaically tries. Almost no of the decency that we find on the planet could be practiced without persuasion."

However, the decency of persuasion and the way that it is implanted inside human instinct isn't what causes individuals' concern. What causes nervousness if the corruption of persuasion. Certainly, when persuasion is contorted, it can get manipulative, which is perilous. Through control, extortionists, clique pioneers, and despots have manhandled, subjugated, and even massacred millions. In any case, as impeding as control may be, it ought to never be mistaken for persuasion. Control is the depravity of persuasion. It isn't worried about truth, but instead duplicity. Aristotle remarked on this in his acclaimed work, Rhetoric when he emphasized, "an abuse of the explanatory workforce can work incredible mischief; a similar charge can be brought against every single beneficial thing spare virtue itself, and particularly against the most helpful things, for example, quality, wellbeing, riches, and military aptitude. Appropriately utilized, they work the best gift; and wrongly utilized, they work the best harm."

Chapter 16 How Manipulation Works

B efore we dive deep, it is vital that we define the meaning of manipulation. When you consider manipulation based on psychology, you will interpret it as a social influence that changes the actions, perceptions of others using deceptive and hidden tactics.

The manipulator will work to improve their interests at the expense of others. A lot of tactics used by manipulators are considered abusive, devious, and deceptive. Although social influence isn't negative, when a person or group is being manipulated, it has the potential to harm them.

Social influence, such as a doctor trying to persuade a patient to start practicing healthy habits is considered harmless. This is true of any social influence that respects the rights of those required to decide and is not unduly coercive. On the flip side, if a person is attempting to get their own way and is taking advantage of people by going against their will, the social influence can have a negative impact and is generally undermined.

Emotional or psychological manipulation is considered as a form of coercion and persuasion. There are a lot of components that can be employed in this type of mind control, such as brainwashing and bullying.

In most cases, people will consider this as abusive or deceptive. Those who decide to manipulate will do so to try to control the actions of those around them. The manipulator will have some targets in mind and will apply various abuse forms to persuade those around them into assisting the manipulator to achieve the target. For the most part, emotional blackmail will be used.

Those who manipulate other people use mind control, bullying and many other methods to make others do what they want

The person being manipulated may not want to do the task, but since they will feel like they have no other alternative because of blackmail or the tactic employed. Many people that are manipulative lack the right caring and sensitivity towards others so they may not see a problem with their actions.

Some manipulators are only interested in achieving their end goal and don't care who has been hurt in the process. Additionally, manipulative people fear to get into a healthy relationship because they are afraid that others will not accept them. A person with a manipulative personality will always have the weakness of taking responsibility for their own problems, life, and behavior. Since they cannot take responsibility for issues that may arise, the manipulator will apply manipulation tactics to get someone else to own their responsibility.

Manipulators usually borrow tactics in other forms of mind control to attain the influence they want in others. One of the most popular tactics is called emotional blackmail. For this tactic, the manipulator will strive to motivate guilt or sympathy in the person they are manipulating. These two emotions are selected because they are the strongest of all human emotions and are the most likely to trigger others to do what the manipulator wants. The manipulator will then take complete advantage of the person, using the guilt they have to persuade others into helping them attain their end goal.

Usually, the manipulator will not only build these emotions, but they will also trigger some level of guilt that is out of proportion for the situation taking place. This implies that they can take an instance like missing out on a party appears like a person is missing out on funeral or something vital.

Emotional blackmail is just one of the strategies used by manipulators. Another successful tactic is a type of abuse known as crazy-making. This tactic is used with the hope of building self-doubt in the person being manipulated. Typically, this self-doubt will become very strong that some people may begin to feel like they are going crazy. Sometimes, the manipulator will apply passive-aggressive behavior to generate crazy-making. They may also decide to support or approve the subject verbally, but again show non-verbal cues that contradict what they said. The manipulator will usually try to undermine specific events while loudly supporting the same behavior.

In case the manipulator is caught ready handed, they will deny, justify, or deceive to get out of trouble. One of the biggest challenges with psychological manipulators is that they are slow to learn the needs of people around them. This does not support the behavior they are doing, but others needs are not factored so they can manipulate others without feeling any shame.

Also, the manipulator may find it hard to create long-lasting and meaningful friendships because the people they are with will always feel used and have issues trusting the manipulator.

Requirements to successfully manipulate

A successful manipulator must have tactics at hand that will help them succeed at persuading people to achieve their own end goal.

Simon says that the manipulator will require to:

1. Hide their aggressive behaviors and intentions from the person or people they want to manipulate.

2. Determine the weaknesses of their intended subject or victims to identify the tactics that will be most ideal in achieving their goals.

3. Develop some degree of ruthlessness so that they will not handle any doubts that arise because of harming the subjects if it arrives at that. This harm can either be emotional or physical.

The first thing that the manipulator has to fulfill to manipulate others successfully is to hide their aggressive behaviors and intentions. This means that if the manipulator starts to tell people of their plans, no one is going to stay for long to be manipulated. Instead, the manipulator requires safeguarding their thoughts from others and behaving like everything is usual. Usually, the subjects being manipulated will no know about it, at least not at the start. The manipulator will be friendly, act like their best friend, and probably help them out with some problem or another. By the time the people become aware of the issue, the manipulator has sufficient information about them to use it to coerce them into moving forward.

This can assist them in figuring out the kind of tactics that they can apply to attain their overall goal.

Sometimes the manipulator can manage to complete this step through a little observation while other times, they will require to have some level of interaction with the people before developing the complete plan.

The third requirement is that the manipulator has to be ruthless. Things will not go well if the manipulator does his work and then starts to worry about how the subject is going to fair in the end. If they care about the subject, the chances are that they will not apply this plan. The manipulator has to stop caring about the subject; they should not care if any harm, either physical or emotional, occurs on the subject as long as the overall goal is realized.

One of the reasons why manipulators succeed is that the subject is not aware that they are being manipulated until later on in the process. They may think that everything is going on well; maybe they think that they have found a new friend in the manipulator. By the time the subject discovers that they are being taken advantage, they are stuck. The manipulator will manage to apply all tactics, including emotional blackmail, to realize their end goal.

The motivating feature in manipulative interaction

Right now you are aware that a significant characteristic of manipulative interaction is the realization that the "deliberate action" is the right choice for him in a certain situation. The ability of the manipulator to change the critical capacity to destroy the judgment may interfere with the awareness of the target, but it doesn't result in the change of direction.

This means that blurring and clouding affecting the critical capacity does not stimulate the "desirable" track. A strong incentive is needed to ensure that deliberate action is the first in the target's scale of choice. To realize this effect, the manipulator requires creating a link between the intentional action and the achievement of a powerful wish.

For the most part, the manipulator awakens a strong force in the subject's mind. He builds the notion that fulfillment can be attained if the target sticks to the instructions of the manipulator. The motivating factor in manipulative interaction shows a gap between the manipulator and the target. The target is trying to realize a powerful wish while the manipulator encourages him to do it by using incentives that create a false impression.

Manipulation as a motivating behavior

Manipulation is a motivating action. It is an effort by a person to make his or her colleague behave in a certain way, and for a certain purpose. The decision to manipulate and not apply a direct technique shows that the participants in the interaction have opposing stands. Robert Godin, in his Manipulator Politics, lists and criticizes a neo-Marxist view that describes the contradiction results from various interests. Manipulation basically works against the interest of those being manipulated. From this perspective, it is implicit that any encouraging action that is applied for the advantage of the target could never be part of the manipulation. This means the neo-Marxist view excludes the entire side of partially positive manipulations that are concentrated to progress the target's interests. Godin, who attempts to suggest an enhanced approach to the study of manipulative behavior, considers that the contradiction is facilitated by various wills and not essentially by contradicting interests, that is "One person—causing the other to act contrary to his putative will."

Godin's definition, which concentrates on contradictory wills, considers that the target's will, or at least his putative will, is always open to the manipulator. Usually enough, but, human beings like to speak in a different and contradictory voice simultaneously, which makes it difficult to understand what they really want. Does that imply that they cannot be manipulated?

Consider this, the rich housewife who keeps complaining that the maintenance task causes her to feel miserable, frustrated and unhappy, but she refuses to employ someone to help her. How could we forget to talk about the miserable Don Juan, who wants to get married, but constantly has love affairs only with married women? And perhaps there is the tragic example of the excellent musician who dedicated most of her life to learning the art of opera but keeps avoiding wonderful opportunities to audition in front of popular conductors who could be able to assist her to expand her professional career.

These three tragic heroes-the miserable housewives frustrated Don Juan, and the desperate musician is great examples that ambiguity regarding a person's intention will originate from the fact that he himself is confused and cannot make a decision. Ironically, manipulative interference can be useful in assisting the struggler to understand his will and arrive at a decision. Indeed, so many techniques in psychotherapy and education are designed to assist a confused person to discover his purpose and choose what to do with it.

The definition of Godin also appears problematic in scenarios where the manipulator and the target tend to share the same objectives. In those particular associations, the motivation to apply a manipulative approach can be pushed by different objectives on opportunities to complete the will, such as in the case where the target is in need to satisfy his will and realize his goals.

Now, we can look at Goodin's definition like an indirect move that is executed out of fear that a direct approach will face opposition.

Chapter 17 Communication Skills

I t is possible that after reading this you have found that your nonverbal communication skills are lacking. There are absolutely different activities that you can do to help him prove what you are saying to others. Taking the time to spend a few minutes a day working on your nonverbal communication can lead to a more successful life. This is because people will understand how you're truly feeling and thinking as you tried to express yourself to them.

You find the taking a few minutes out of your day to think about your facial expressions can work in your favor. Some people have a very hard time controlling their expression and this can make others uncomfortable when they are not interested or object to the things that are being said. Being aware of the look on your face can help set people at ease. In addition, it will help them trust you more and listen to the things that you have to say.

Another thing that can help you to improve your nonverbal communication is to pay attention to how you act. When you are standing in a room and talking with somebody how close are you standing to them? Giving them more or less space can help improve the communication between you. Remember to close is not good, however, too far away is also not good. There is a fun experiment that you can try where two people stand fairly far apart and two steps at a time come closer and closer together. When one person starts to feel uncomfortable, they raise their hand to tell the other to stop. This gives you a good look at what most people's personal space is.

As noted, working on your tone and inflection can also improve your communication. Alongside of this is eye contact. Many people struggle with the right amount of eye contact and it can make you seem shifty.

Practicing these things together can improve overall communication skills. This goes for both verbal and nonverbal skills.

People who effectively communicate verbally and non-verbally tend to have higher levels of self-esteem. This is because they truly feel understood. The people around them can listen to them talk and gain true insight from them. This is great for businesses and personal lives. Taking the time to work on your communication skills can absolutely help to improve your life, overall.

Opening up your stance and relaxing a bit can help improve the confidence that you have in yourself. It can make talking with others much easier. An open stance will naturally make you more relaxed and approachable. You won't be as afraid to talk to those people that are coming up to you as they will also be relaxed because of your stance.

When people are coming up to you and talking it's going to encourage you to talk back. Being aware of how you look and what you are saying well, naturally make you feel more confident. Taking notice to small twitches that might show nervousness and correcting them will also make you more confident. Self-esteem can be built quite easily, and your communication skills will play a major role in it. When you decide to start working on yourself and trying to like yourself more focusing on your verbal and nonverbal communication will certainly help you along the way.

Some of you folks may be exceptionally confident when talking to an individual person or small crowds. However, when you get in front of a large crowd as it can be increasingly more intimidating Training yourself to be confident and have great self-esteem can be difficult in a situation where there are thousands of people listening to you. Remembering that your body language speaks just as loud as your words will help you when put in these situations. When you are able to relate to the thousands of people looking at you and they are able to relate to you it will truly help build you up.

On the other side of that many people are great at talking to a group of people but on an individual level they struggle. Talking one-on-one or with a very small group of people can be emotionally intimidating. It can make someone feel as if they have to be more vulnerable than they want to be. This goes along with the eyes being the window to the soul. We tend to be in closer proximity when working with only one person or a small group of people. They will be able to more easily see what's going on with you while you talk.

Most people have at least one person they are comfortable talking with. It is great practice to spend time with that person and see how you react while in a one-on-one situation. Paying special attention to the tone of your voice, your body language, your eyes, and your facial expressions can lead you to more confidence when dealing with people you are not so comfortable with. Practicing talking to small groups or two people that are not necessarily your best friends is the best course of action and learning how to be confident in these situations. As with all things, practice truly does make perfect.

There is a ton a different activity that can be used on an individual or group basis to help with communication. Many companies throughout the world use them frequently to ensure that their team understands how well they communicate with each other. Finding these different activities is exceptionally simple. If you are looking for ways for your team to build better communication, I know that there are many resources out there that can help you.

Chapter 18 Technics To Influence Other

All of us live different lives, and there may be those of you out in your own community who go into battle every day. Therefore, here is a list of all the known persuasive methods that masters use to manipulate and get what they want.

Nonetheless, please note that great responsibility comes with high energy. Always use your experience and not just your own for the good of everyone. You're having that, Spidey?

How to Cooperate with People

Humour-You makes people feel good if you can make them laugh. This allows you to build a relationship with them quickly.

Smile-First impressions last, and first impressions with a smile are a benefit. Try to smile at every person in the street.

Respect-We all know that it is appreciated and not hated. Firstly, however, you should always thank everyone you encounter. It's still convenient for someone who loves you to do a favor.

Create quick connections-people who can immediately make contact with someone have more friends and can build good relationships than people who can't.

Using body Language-Body language awareness is included in the program. Our regular contact is 55% body language. Although the people you talk with interpret the signals instinctively, learning how to identify such messages is an asset in the art of persuasion.

The Halo Effect–Generally, we classify people as good or generally evil. Any characteristic that you will show a person in the future can be influenced by what you teach today. Make sure anybody you meet today feels like you're usually right.

Similarity-Same feathered birds, don't they flock together? If you can always find a way to understand what is shared between you and the other person instantly, you can quickly build a connection. This relationship eventually becomes faith, which is always what people have to do for you.

Goodwill-Be genuine always if you show interest in others. Being frank about your concern for others will make them quicker like you.

Bonding–The names of people sound to their ears like jingle bells. Address people by name and they will pay more attention to you.

The methods of mirroring and matching Mirror your language–Mirroring is a technique used for neurological programming to create relationships with an individual unconsciously. Using the same language, the other person uses will help you build this relationship in no time.

Match your breathing–breathing alone can help you create a link that you are convinced to use. The effectiveness of this method is dependent on its disguise. Who will ever know that somebody is trying to copy their practice of breathing?

Match the Tone-Matching, the voice of a person, operates on an unconscious level as you see all the mirrored techniques here.

Mirror their moods–If your partner is in a bad mood, are you jokingly approaching them? Of course not of course not just assess the attitude of people until you do what you want.

Test your energy level–The energy level of a person can tell you how likely you are to make suggestions. If you can be as cheerful or as energetic as they are, you can lead them to your plans much faster.

Cognitive dissonance test

Create relationships–If you are able to get people to commit, this person will most likely do what you asked them to do. You will have a sense of uncomfortably that will last for some time if you don't.

Using written Obligations-Written promises are better than oral ones. It can also function as a bond between you and the other person.

Build public commitments-public commitments are even better than written promises. There will be not only a concern for the relationship but also the integrity of the individual.

Using external rewards-business, people always use their workers ' incentives. Although the inspiration it provides lasts only for a short time, it still does the job.

Always make them say "Yes" –This is a kind of conditioning in which the response of the person is matched by the stimulus that you offer in this case.

Make a concerted effort–if you can get people to make an effort, they will more likely stick to your plans or execute their requests.

Create dissonance and offer a solution-just take care to provide a way out if you plan to make someone feel uncomfortable to get them to do as you like.

Create a sense of obligation

Present Giving-How do you feel about giving a gift to someone and you've got nothing to give back? Very bad, isn't it? You'll probably say, "Geez, don't you have anything. Just let me know if you need anything..."

Mutual compromise–Often, people will try to influence their minds, so that you may feel helpless when you know that you don't agree with what just happened. Don't worry! Don't worry! What the other person does not know is that when it is your turn to make him / her consent to your application, he or she is just as weak.

Give a favor, get it back-people do things for you sometimes, whether you like it or not. The problem is that it induces a need to reciprocate in the mind of the receiver. If you are a generous person who is happy to give favours to others without anything in return, simply make sure you let them know.

Sharing secrets-Share the secret to building a bond, a sense of duty, and a sense of trust Just note, the secrets that you share depend on the type of person with whom you share them.

Group power think

Build a team-The The more extensive the band, the better. Human beings have a substantial socializing need. People join groups to have a sense of belonging. If you want people to live up to your values, reinforce the community, and develop it.

Familiarize everyone-if you can get people to identify strongly with your party, it will be easier to influence their actions. Make sure everybody is the same as they think.

Set the values—companies typically have beliefs that they bring together in the form of mission and vision statements. Such costs need to be adhered to by people within the organization or group.

The Persuasion Language

Using repeated language-avoid using offensive words and replacing them with less offensive ones. For example: use mentally challenged rather than communication, idiot, propaganda, instead of torture, enhanced interrogation, etc.

Play with Numbers-Play with numbers while you illustrate something to convince. Seek anything like, "close to nine in ten" or "less than five in all..." 38. Using positive words— what you want is for people to feel comfortable and confident in what they want. So, when you try to communicate, use positive words.

Words with emotion–Words filled with emotions are incredibly helpful for people to behave. Only look at how the term "terrorism" was used by George W. Bush in his war against the enemies of America. Be quiet-the best thing to do after making a contract is to be silent. The person has already chosen, and you won't want to ruin the whole thing by giving the other man contradictory ideas by accident.

Painting images with Words-Isn't it nice to walk around the park with the beautiful trees all over the place, swinging back and forth to the fresh air? You can only feel the morning sun's rays hit your soft skin softly before you stand on a pile of dog poo (Hey! We just smash you. We're not even in the middle of the list)

Choose the right words-The the right words will make a big difference sometimes. Instead of uttering, "Sir, I'm very sure we will have difficulty convincing your staff." Try this, "Sir, I am sure the workers will appreciate it and will give you more support if we try other forms." Replace "you" with "let's"–more people will participate by replacing "let's" with "you." The term "let us" gives you a sense of engagement. So from now on, let's try using "let's."

Use simple statements-In simple, direct, and short statements; give your instructions. It's easier not only to remember but also to understand and absorb.

Use your everyday language-your listeners and/or readers will only be fooled by complicated language. You have an enormous vocabulary, definitely, but if you speak like an intellectually dexterous (geek) person all the time, you will be misinterpreted more likely.

Avoid vulgar words and curse words-try to prevent profanity in your comments (especially new acquaintances) as far as possible. Your reputation depends most of the time on the sort of terms you use.

Avoid jargon, and technical Language-There is no problem when the person you talk to works in the same field you are in. Nonetheless, you communicate with different people in most situations.

Keep phrases brief—A single phrase can stand as a whole in the early centuries. Today, we clearly live in a world where a single word like "party" is sufficient to say it all. This said, "Let's" "run."

Don't beat around the bush-say it clearly if you have something to say.

Using words—Words in speech are more likely to move people. Keep in mind that your words are conceived by the person with whom you speak. Thought takes precedence over motion.

Terms like Free, Easy, Earn Now, Sexy, And Guaranteed are just a few of the other attentiveness terms that you can use. Try to Experiment these words in your statements.

Highlight what you want-look at the last sentence above.

Pace—Research has shown that speaking faster is more persuasive than talking slowly and monotonously.

Avoid vocal Fillers-What does this mean... Uhm to make ...Uhm your thoughts accepted. When speaking, don't use these kinds of words.

Determine your pitch-it has been more effective for convincing speech to lower the pitch of your voice.

Change the Voice-Speak loud enough to listen to you. Check the sound system first if you speak to a crowd so that the audience doesn't end up being deaf during your speech.

Be more 'concise—concepts conveyed easily and regularly add credibility. People will most likely respond to your questions or orders if they can understand fully what you want to say.

Taking a while to take a break— emphasis does not mean that you should talk louder, more quickly, in a low voice, etc. Sometimes you have to pause so that people have time to digest what you just said.

Chapter 19 Psychological Manipulation Techniques

S ome manipulators are so hazardous that they could inflict so deep wounds that may take a long time to heal.

When you meet a charming person, it is not always applicable that they may be a sociopath, but if you feel that you are being gas lighted, manipulated or messed up with an excessively loving person, then this could be possible that the charming personality is none other than a sociopath. Sociopaths are the people who are people who know how to manipulate people so well that they have a way of controlling others around them be it any situation. They would know every tiny bit of you from the way you dress to your mental ability to think.

The main target of manipulators is the people who are vulnerable and easy to dominate. They judge you and then play with your emotions accordingly. Being in touch with a sociopath could be a disorienting experience for you, once you know all their tactics and games they play, you would not let them take over your advantage.

Here are some major mind manipulating games, that manipulators play-

1) Flattering You Extensively-

It is a fact that everyone who flatters enormously is not a sociopath, it depends. But in case they are a sociopath, they would do whatever it takes to win you over your trust, and gain your confidence. If you know about this strategy of them prior, you may not become a target of these manipulators and would know in advance that the compliments and flattering remarks given by them are in-genuine.

The manipulators like these may say that 'you are the most amazing person, humble, charming, or intelligent person on this planet that I have ever met' or 'my life is incomplete without you'. Even though it has not been long that you have met that person, in those cases, if statements like these are being used it may be a hint or indication for you understand.

2) Never Take Accountability for Anything-

Usually, manipulators never take any kind of responsibility for their decisions, feelings or behavior. Instead of being accountable for their actions, they blame others for such actions. However, the other person would want to make the situation better and would not even know that it was not their fault, but they are being targeted by the sociopaths. They will comply with all the demands issued by manipulators as they would feel insecure for such actions and in respect to bringing the situation at peace.

3) Enjoy In Messing You Up-

Manipulators may enjoy messing with your head. They will not show any contrition even for their mistakes. Instead of showing remorse, they will blame you and will take pleasure in doing so. For example- if you quarrel with your friend for any reason, the manipulator will take advantage of that situation by acting sympathetic and taking your side. He will criticize and highlight how awfully your friend treated you. This is one of the manipulative behaviors that sociopaths play with other people. Now that you are aware, you may not get caught up in their manipulating strategies.

4) Have a Full Control-

Biggest manipulators play the manipulation games by keeping control over the other person. They would always turn the situation in their way and always want the ball in their court. If things are not going the way they want, they start argumentation and show aggression. They may even threaten you at some points as they start dominating you.

Some manipulators use 'threats of suicide' or some may say 'you will feel sorry for what you did.

5) Lying and Cheating-

It is one of the common and blatant signs of a manipulator. The manipulators just want to reach their goal and always want to achieve what they have thought of, no matter what may come. Lying to a person or cheating on them is their biggest tool to take over your advantage. The sociopaths will not follow usual codes of conduct as that is why they are manipulators, so you have to be assertive to find out their 'not so good' games that they play and have that gut to feel the vibes of the other person is negative.

6) Gas lighting Your Opponent-

It is one of the dark tactics that many manipulators use to confuse you, you feel like you can't win the argument after being gas lighted by the manipulator. It is something in which manipulators use your words against you even if you haven't said anything wrong or no matter how authentically you are doing something. They will let question your sanity and you will defend yourself ending up saying statements like 'I did not mean that way' or 'I am sorry if you felt bad'. They will make you feel guilty for what you have done (even if you were not at invalid). They would also provoke you through immoral actions and disturbing statements and then pretend to be over-emotional or sensitive, and irrational.

7) Manipulators Always Play On Your Good Side-

Sociopaths always find and discover your weaknesses and kindness against something. They then use those weaknesses against you and find the reasons which will give you a benefit of doubt which makes you an easy target.

8) Make You Lose Your Self-Belief Power-

Manipulators do certain things which may loosen up your morality and rationality such as not letting you speak up against anyone, make you lose your confidence, questing yourself about your existence, assert boundaries and degrading your self-esteem. And after a certain period, it becomes very hard to negotiate from within that relation without abuse or offending, or displeasing further confrontation.

9) Justifying the Immorality Done By Them-

They would justify all their actions. Even if they break the law, they would rationalize it. Manipulators only focus on their needs, they are not concerned about anything else if their needs are getting fulfilled and they are getting benefit out of it even if it is illegal. If you try to make them realize about their mistake, they would cover it up by manipulating your reaction against that situation. They will turn your mind the way that you will start feeling whatever has been done by them was not immoral and maybe you are overthinking. One thing is universal with all manipulators that they would never admit about anything they have done illegally. Instead of admitting and feeling guilty, they will make that illegal thing authentic and will justify the reason behind doing that action.

10) Back-Tracked Their Own Words-

A manipulator is not a man of his words. They will never be up to what they say which is enough to make you crazy as you will tell them about what they said and they will pretend that they have never said any such thing ever Moreover, they will enforce your mind to rethink and will make you fall under a doubt that they have never said such a thing what you were thinking.

11) Give You a Silent Treatment-

Some manipulators may play silent games with you. If they want to abandon some action before you do one or they are upset with you regarding some action, they will neither say anything nor make any eye contact with you. Manipulators do not care whether the other person is ethical, they are self-centered and only care about their feelings. The silence is their way of attacking and making you feel guilty regardless you are right or wrong.

12) Bully Intellectually-

A manipulator may also try to use some technical facts and figures which may not even be true just to win an argument with the other person. If they use facts and figures against the topic you already know about, they won't be able to make you wordless so the manipulator would know that against what topic to use the statistics to make you dumbstruck.

13) Treating You Differently-

If a person is having a bad reputation with the others and they are being over-friendly and deeply emotional with you, then something may be dubious. If you are experiencing the same thing with a person, it may be a warning indication to be cautious. For example- if a person is not having a good reputation in the office and just because of that they are being over-friendly with you. You need to be aware of how and why they are treating you differently and analyze the kind of interactions they are initializing with you at the beginning. You can judge and keep distance with them accordingly.

It may not be true all the times as a person may be good to someone, but he may not be good to the other one. You cannot judge a person's behavior based on the other person's verdict. You can just be certain about it once you start getting familiar to that person. And yes, certainly, now that you are cognizant of all the manipulation games played by sociopaths with the other person to dominate, execute and take over the advantage of them, you will not let them do so. Manipulators cannot harm you until you are acquainted with all their dark psychological tactics.

Sociopaths think that this is their biggest strength to manipulate people and this is what they use against the innocent ones. But if you can spot their signs, this will keep you safe as well as transform their biggest strength into a weakness.

Chapter 20 Techniques Of Manipulation In Life

Have you ever noticed that the most successful people are also the most persuasive? In the workplace, it is rarely the aggressive bossy people that rise to the top. Great leaders have a knack of making other people feel better about them and achieve better results. Use the following techniques to become a better manipulator both at work and at home.

- Inspire confidence

Do you give compliments regularly? Are you quick to praise people when they achieve their goals? If not, then why not? A few words can go a long way to boost someone's confidence. Make sure you tell people when they have done a good job and encourage them to greater things.

Once you master this technique and feel comfortable giving praise this will spill over into your personal life. If your partner looks sensational then tell them! If your kids have done well at school, then reward them with your praise.

Quick tip: Only give sincere compliments and do not use them to play people. If you are using manipulation to avoid tasks at work you will soon get a reputation for using people.

- Repetition

Many people believe that passion alone can make an idea stand out amid a sea of other ideas. This is not true and successful people realize that the key to standing out in societies information overload is repetition. We have all developed filters to protect us from the bombardment of information in this media led world and need to hear something multiple times before it sinks in. If you have a great idea and voice it to someone make sure you follow up with a written version.

- Deliver your message in context

Too often we are tempted to make ourselves look more intelligent by using technical jargon or abstract references. You will achieve much better results if you tune into your audience's frame of mind. Avoid terms that are non-specific. If you have an idea to make things "easier to use" or "better and quicker" then state how much easier or how much better and quicker

- Personalize your message

Statements of fact can often be bland and uninteresting. If you can personalize your speech you have a greater impact on your audience. This is a great tool at work, if you are approaching someone who is creative then tailor your speech to reflect this.

This technique will also help your social life. Whenever you are meeting new people try and do a bit of homework so you know more about them.

- Use your contacts

Everyone is more open to people who they believe have mutual associations. Your connections can help you progress and providing you don't abuse their influence they can aid your progress at work. Your credibility can rise with the relevance of your contacts and friends.

- Use visualization techniques

Have you noticed that the most successful sales pitches have a strong visual element? Picture Apples Steve Jobs and you can visualize the stage and the graphics that he used to get his message across. Even his clothes became part of the whole message that Apple was trying to convey.

Not everyone will be able to comprehend what you see in your mind's eye, especially if they have less knowledge in the domain you represent.

- Social media

Do you use social media to its full potential? Are you prepared to invest time and energy in your online connections? If not, then you are missing a huge opportunity. The potential to reach thousands of people who can help you in your career is invaluable.

Potential investors or customers are all waiting for you to tell your story or promote your product. Social media allows you to solicit ideas from a huge audience all with the click of a mouse. The power of a "like button" is not to be ignored! The evidence of thousands of positive affirmations will only serve to amplify your voice and make more people listen.

Your social life can also thrive online. Groups of like-minded people are all out there waiting for you to join them. Maybe you have a passion for sailing or extreme sports but aren't sure of the facilities near you. Facebook is a great place to start looking for groups in your area, reach out and connect. Use Twitter and Instagram to help your dating life if you are looking for love! Providing you take precautions and always meet for the first time in public you can meet some interesting people!

Quick tip: Social media can also be a brutal place and it is essential you monitor your settings. Before you join a group makes sure they can only see the information you are comfortable with.

- Listen intently

If you want to get someone to like you the best way is to let them talk about themselves. Adopt a relaxed posture and allow them to tell you all about themselves. Show genuine interest and ask pertinent questions as you listen.

What is the common factor all these questions have?

"That is fascinating, how did you manage that?"

"Interesting, do you have any examples of what you mean?"

"Your knowledge about……. Is amazing, what do you think about…?"

They are all questions that elicit a response. This shows the speaker that you are not just listening, but you have a genuine interest in what they are saying. You are also allowing the speaker to expand the conversation and this creates a bond between the two of you. They will see you as an ally and a person they can trust.

Persuasion and manipulation are both powerful forces that can be used to make your life better. Ethical communications help others and make them a part of your team.

Chapter 21 Emotional Manipulation Tactics

Once a person understands the power of emotions, he/she can use it ethically or unethically. The last thing that we want is having someone manipulating our emotions, whether it is a friend, colleague, or politician. There are some ways through which a master manipulator can use emotional intelligence against you. Please note that not everyone who has the characteristics listed below and used the said skill has selfish intentions. Some people practice them with no intended harm. Nonetheless, having an increased awareness of these behaviors will empower you to deal with manipulators strategically and sharpen your intelligence quotient in the process.

1. Manipulators play on fear.

Majority of manipulators will overemphasis specific points and exaggerate facts in an effort to make you scared and have you acting as they want. The way to identify this play is by looking out for statements that imply you are not strong or courageous enough or that if you miss out on a particular thing, you are a loser.

2. Manipulators deceive

Everybody values honesty and transparency thus will avoid deceivers. Manipulators understand this concept and are very cunning when lying. They twist the facts or try to show you only the side of the story that benefits them. For instance, a work colleague can spread some unconfirmed rumor to gain an upper hand. To avoid being deceived, do not believe everything you hear. Instead, base your choices on credible sources and ask questions if the details are not clear.

3. Manipulators take advantage of your happiness

Have you noticed that you are more likely to say yes to anything when you are happy or in a good mood? When we are happy, we tend to jump on opportunities that look good even before we think things through. Master manipulators have this knowledge thus will take advantage of the moods. To manage this emotional opportunity and avoid manipulation, work to improve awareness of your emotions, both positive and negative. Strive to strike a balance between logic and emotions when making decisions.

4. Manipulators take advantage of reciprocity.

Do you know that feeling you get when you owe someone a favor especially if they helped you at one point? That feeling of debt makes one vulnerable. It is hard to say no to a manipulator if you owe them something. Most of the manipulators will attempt to butter and flatter you with small favors then ask for a big one in return. As much as giving brings more joy than receiving, it is more important to know your limits. Do not be afraid to say no when you have to even if you owe someone a favor.

5. Manipulators push for a home court advantage

It is very easy to convince a person when you are in a familiar place. As such, a manipulator will push you towards meeting you in a place he/she is familiar with while you are not. Ownership gives power and comfort thus a place like home or the office will give the manipulator some authority. You will have to make requests for meeting in a neutral place where familiarity and ownership are diluted so as to disarm the manipulator.

6. The manipulator will ask a lot of questions.

Naturally, it is easy to talk about oneself. Master manipulators know this thus they take advantage to ask some probing questions. Their agendas are hidden but basically, they seek to discover your weaknesses or other information they can hold against you. Of course, it would be unfair for you to assume that everyone has wrong motives because there are a few people who genuinely seek to know you better. However, it is okay to question people, especially those who reveal nothing about themselves.

7. The manipulator will speak quickly

In order to manipulate you through your emotions, the manipulator will speak quickly and sometimes use jargon and special vocabulary. This will give them an advantage because you will not have enough time to think. Fry you to counter this form of manipulation; do not feel afraid to ask for some time to process what the person said. Also, make a point of asking the person to repeat any unclear statements. To gain some control of a conversation, repeat the points the other person makes in your own words and let them sink.

8. The display of negative emotions

Some manipulators will use voice tones to control your emotions. The most commonly used tone and body language by manipulators are negative. For instance, basketball coaches (they use manipulation for positive purposes) are masters at raising their voices and using strong body language to manipulate the emotions of the players. To avoid such manipulation, you should practice pausing. It involves taking a break from the conversation or situation and having some time to think before reacting. In fact, you may walk away for some minutes to get a grip of your own emotions.

9. Manipulators limit your time to act

Basically, every manipulator wants to win. They may do this by ensuring that you do not have enough time to think. For instance, an individual may force you to make a serious decision in an unreasonably limited amount of time. He/she will try to steer your thoughts to their advantage. You will not have enough time to weigh the consequences. To avoid a situation where you give in without thought, do not be in a rush to submit. Ensure that the demand is reasonable. Take the pause, ask for some time, and if the person does not allow you to think, walk away. You will be happier looking for whatever you need elsewhere.

10. The silent treatment.

According to Preston Ni, a manipulator will presume power in a relationship by making you wait. For instance, when a person deliberately fails to respond to your reasonable messages, calls, emails, or other inquiries, he/she makes you wait and at the same time, places uncertainty and doubt in your mind. Some manipulators use silence as leverage. To avoid being a victim of manipulation through silent treatment, give people deadlines and do not allow them to intimidate you. For instance, after attempting to communicate to a reasonable degree, let go of the mater and let the other person reach out.

Manipulators will work to increase their emotional awareness so as to have an upper hand on others. In fact, a large number of people are learning how to be emotionally intelligent. You too should seek to sharpen your emotional intelligence levels, for your own protection.

Chapter 22 Manipulation Games

You have heard of mind games. You have surely played them before and had them played on you. You can use mind games as an effective persuasion tool when you know what to do and when. There are numerous techniques that are effective, and they are not that difficult to learn. This means that once you know what they are, you can start utilizing mind games right away to start getting what you want.

Kick Me

This likely reminds you of that game when you were a kid where you put a sign on someone's back that read "kick me." This is similar. You want to make yourself look like someone that deserves pity. Once you get pity from someone, it is easier to get them to do what you want. You can use this for just about anything in life from getting someone to allow you to apologize to getting a boss to give you a promotion once you get really good at it.

Now That I've Got You

This is a game that you will use when you want to show a person you are winning and better. You can also use it when you are angry and want to justify it. For example, your friend had a party, but he neglected to invite you. So, you decide to host a party the following weekend with the intent to just not invite him. This game basically has you working to one up another person to get them to give in and give you what you want.

You Made Me Do It

This is another one you used during childhood and you likely did not even realize at the time that it was a type of mind game. This is a game that works to make another person feel guilty while simultaneously absolving you of any responsibility for your actions. For example, you want to be left alone. However, someone comes in the room to ask you a question. As a result, you are startled and drop your beverage. You tell that person that they made you drop your beverage.

If It Weren't for You

This is another mind game that is used to absolve yourself of any guilt for something you might have done. With this type of game, you essentially create a scenario that allows you to put guilt onto someone. This gives you an array of advantages. When a person is feeling guilty about something, they are more vulnerable to suggestion. For example, you are unable to go to work for whatever reason. You find a way to blame your spouse for this and make them feel guilty. As a result, you are able to coerce your spouse into making you a meal or buying you something.

Let You Both Fight

The purpose of this mind game is to share blame, control other people and even make you seem like a good friend. In most cases, this is a mind game that women will play, but it is becoming more common among men. For example, a person knows that two people are attracted to them. This person then talks both of the interested parties into fighting with one another to basically win their heart. This is basically a type of transaction; however, at the end of the game, both interested parties are usually left without anyone.

RAPO

This mind game can be a major ego boost, give a sense of satisfaction and increase how desirable you see yourself to be. It is a type of social game in which you essentially convince a person to pursue you. You convince them in a way that is not obvious to them, so they do not even know what it is happening. How you choose to convince them is flexible and really dependent on your preferences and what it takes to get into the subconscious of the person you are seeking to lure. What is good about this game is that it generally does not take long to put into practice.

Perversion

The purpose of this game is to avoid responsibility and garner sympathy. Basically, this mind game is used to seduce another person. You cause them to feel guilty if they are not fulfilling your romantic needs. You talk about a bad past relationship, whether it was real or not, to first get sympathy from them. Then, once they essentially soften to the idea of fulfilling your desires, you go in and take what you want. If they are still resistant, you cause them to feel guilty to ultimately get what you want.

Clever Me

This one improves your identity, social capital, attention and ego. You do something to show someone what you are great at and you want the entire world to know that you are awesome at this specific thing. You manipulate the situation to make sure that someone will learn about your skill. You get attention from them and they tell others. Before you know it, your skill or talent is being spread around and a lot of people are coming to you to pay you a compliment.

Wooden Leg

This is a game people play for sympathy, as a plea of insanity or to avoid responsibility. You have likely heard the saying that you can only expect so much from a person who has a wooden leg. This game is built upon this saying. Basically, you use a perceived shortfall or disability to gain sympathy and make your actions seem justified. For example, you just cheated on your spouse and he or she found out. You would say something like, "well, my parents had a bad marriage, so what do you expect of me?" They then start to give you sympathy and you are absolved of your guilt.

The Double Request

This is a common mind game among those who want something big but know that they will not get it just asking for it. For example, you ask for a new expensive watch, but you really want a new jacket that tends to be less expensive. You mention both items, but you make it seem like the watch is what you truly desire. In the end, the friend you are talking to remembers that the jacket was cheaper and also something that you wanted, so they buy it. You end up getting the jacket you wanted from the start.

You're a Good Person

This is a common mind game to play when you want to get something out of someone that they are not normally asked. When you start the conversation by telling them that they are a good person, they are getting recognition and an ego boost from you. This already softens them and makes them more prone to give you exactly what you want. Once you see that their body language is softer or even just neutral, you want to go in and ask for what you want.

Chapter 23 Understand The Various Dark Personalities

Both world history and regular day to day existence are brimming with instances of individuals acting heartlessly, malignantly, or childishly. In psychology just as in ordinary language, we have different names for the different dark inclinations human may have, most conspicuously psychopathy (absence of sympathy), narcissism (over the top self-assimilation), and Machiavellianism (the conviction that whatever it takes to get the job done, so be it), the alleged 'dark group of three,' alongside numerous others, for example, selfishness, perversion, or anger.

Even though from the outset there give off an impression of being critical contrasts between these characteristics - and it might appear to be progressively 'worthy' to be a self-seeker than a mental case - new research shows that every dark part of human character is firmly connected and depends on a similar inclination. That is, most dark qualities can be comprehended as enhanced appearances of a solitary typical essential aura: The dark center of the character. By and by, this suggests if you tend to show one of these mysterious character qualities, you are likewise bound to have a robust inclination to show at least one of the others.

As the new research uncovers, the shared factor of every dark attribute, the D-factor, can be characterized as the general propensity to expand one's utility - ignoring, tolerating, or maliciously inciting disutility for other people -, and joined by convictions that fill in as avocations.

As it was, all dark attributes can be followed back to the general propensity of setting one's objectives and interests over those of others even to the degree of enjoying harming other's - alongside a large group of convictions that fill in as legitimizations and therefore forestall sentiments of blame, disgrace, or something like that. The examination shows that dark attributes when all is said in done can be comprehended as examples of this standard center - even though they may vary in which viewpoints are dominating (e.g., the defenses angle is excellent in narcissism though the part of malignantly inciting disutility is the principle highlight of twistedness). This shared factor is available in nine of the most customarily contemplated dark character characteristics:

• Egoism: an excessive distraction with one's bit of leeway to the detriment of others and the network

• Machiavellianism: a manipulative, hard disposition and a conviction that whatever it takes to get the job done, so is it

• Moral withdrawal: subjective handling style that permits carrying on deceptively without feeling trouble

• Narcissism: unnecessary self-retention, a feeling of predominance, and an extraordinary requirement for consideration from others

• Psychological qualification: a shared conviction that one is superior to other people and merits better treatment

• Psychopathy: the absence of compassion and poise, joined with hasty conduct

• Sadism: a craving to incur mental or physical mischief on others for one's pleasure or to profit oneself

• Self-intrigue: a craving to further and feature one's own social and money related status

• Spitefulness: damaging tendency and readiness to make hurt others, regardless of whether one damage oneself all the while

In a progression of studies with more than 2,500 individuals, the analysts asked to what degree individuals concurred or couldn't help contradicting proclamations, for example, "It is difficult to excel without compromising to a great extent.," "It is at times worth a touch of enduring on my part to see others get the discipline they merit.," or "I realize that I am unique since everybody continues letting me know so." what's more, they considered other self-announced inclinations and practices, for example, hatred or impulsivity and target proportions of narrow-minded and dishonest conduct.

Dark Psychology is both a human awareness development and investigation of the human condition as it identifies with the mental idea of individuals to go after others inspired by psychopathic, freak, or psychopathological criminal drives that need a reason and general suppositions of instinctual drives, developmental science, and sociologies hypothesis. All of humankind has the probability of defrauding people and other living animals. While many control or sublimate this propensity, some follow up on these driving forces. Dark Psychology investigates criminal, freak, and cybercriminal minds.

Dark Psychology is the investigation of the human condition as it identifies with the mental idea of individuals to go after others. All of humanity can mislead different people and living animals. While many control or sublimate this inclination, some follow up on these driving forces. Dark Psychology tries to comprehend those musings, emotions, and discernments that lead to savage human conduct. Dark Psychology expects that this creation is purposive and has some objective, objective arranged inspiration 99.99% of the time. The staying .01%, under Dark Psychology, is the severe exploitation of others without a purposive goal or sensibly characterized by developmental science or a strict authoritative opinion.

Inside the following century, predators and their demonstrations of robbery, viciousness, and misuse will turn into a worldwide wonder and cultural plague if not squashed. Sections of predators incorporate digital stalkers, cyber bullies, digital psychological oppressors, digital lawbreakers, online sexual stalkers, and political/strict devotees occupied with digital fighting. Similarly, as Dark Psychology sees all crook/immoral conduct on a continuum of seriousness and purposive aim, the hypothesis of predator follows a similar structure, yet includes misuse, attack, and online exploitation utilizing Information and Communications Technology. The meaning of iPredator is as per the following:

iPredator

iPredator: An individual, gathering, or country who, legitimately or by implication, participates in misuse, exploitation, pressure, stalking, robbery, or demonization of others utilizing Information and Communications Technology [ICT]. Predators are driven by freak dreams, wants for force and control, revenge, strict enthusiasm, political retaliation, mental disease, perceptual mutilations, peer acknowledgment, or individual and monetary benefit. predators can be any age or sexual orientation and are not bound by financial status, race, religion, or national legacy. iPredator is a common term used to recognize any individual who takes part in criminal, coercive, immoral, or harsh practices utilizing ICT. Key to the development is the reason that Information Age lawbreakers, freaks, and the savagely upset are psychopathological arrangements new to humanity.

Regardless of whether the guilty party is a cyberstalker, digital harasser, cybercriminal, online sexual stalker, web troll, digital fear monger, cyber bully, online kid sex entertainment purchaser/wholesaler, or occupied with web maligning or loathsome online double-dealing, they fall inside the extent of iPredator. The three criteria used to characterize an iPredator include:

• Mindfulness of making hurt others, straightforwardly or in a roundabout way, utilizing ICT.

• The utilization of ICT to get, trade, and convey destructive data.

• A general comprehension of Cyber stealth used to participate in criminal or immoral exercises or to profile, recognize, find, stalk, and draw in an objective.

Not at all like human predators preceding the Information Age, have predators depended upon a large number of advantages offered by Information and Communications Technology [ICT]. These help incorporate trade of data over long separations, rate of data traded, and the interminable access to information accessible. Malignant in aim, predators constantly hoodwink others utilizing ICT in theory and fake electronic universe known as the internet. In this way, as the web offers all ICT clients obscurity, typically, if they choose, predators effectively structure online profiles and diversionary strategies to stay undetected and untraceable.

Arsonist

The Arsonist is an individual with a burning distraction with a fire setting. These people frequently have formative accounts loaded up with sexual and physical maltreatment. Regular among sequential fire playing criminals is the proclivity to be hermits, have scarcely any companions, and captivated by fire and fire setting. Sequential torches are profoundly formal and will, in general, a show designed practices as to their approach for setting fires.

Engrossed by fire setting, Arsonists regularly fantasize and focus upon how to design their fire setting scenes. When their objective is set on fire, a few fire playing criminals experience sexual excitement and continue with masturbation while viewing. Regardless of their obsessive and formal examples, the sequential light playing criminal feels pride in his activities.

Necrophilia

Thanatophobia, Necrophilia, and Necrologies all characterize a similar kind of confused individual. These are individuals, and they do exist, who have a sexual appreciation for bodies. A paraphilia is a biomedical term used to portray an individual's sexual excitement and distraction with items, circumstances, or people that are not part of regulating incitement and may cause trouble or significant issues for the individual. Subsequently, a Necrophile's paraphilia is sexual excitement by an article, a perished individual.

Specialists who have incorporated profiles of Necrophiles demonstrate they have colossal trouble encountering a limit concerning getting physically involved with others. For these individuals, sexual closeness with the dead has a sense of security and security instead of sexual closeness with a living human. Necrophiles have uncovered in interviews feeling an extraordinary feeling of control when in the organization of a corpse. A sense of association gets auxiliary to the essential requirement for saw control.

Chapter 24 Police Manipulation Techniques

All effective actions have the same structure—a sequence of stages—the absence of any of which dramatically (sometimes to zero) reduces the likelihood of success. The impact, built clearly on this structure, is triggered with the greatest possible probability—true, not one hundred percent. The impact, I repeat, refers to any and in any field—in politics, in business, in personal relationships, in sports, in war, in religion. If the effect worked, you are very likely to find a familiar structure in it.

This miracle is called a single impact structure. A single impact structure can be described in two languages, each of which is useful:

- Background lines

- Stages of exposure

Background Lines

So, whatever our goals, if we want to influence another person (or group of people) successfully, we must build three lines of communication:

- Contact line

- Line of distraction

- Line of exposure

Contact Line

Contact is an opportunity for mutual exchange of information. Contact is a desire to perceive each other. Contact is the assumption that communication is more beneficial than ignoring. If there's no contact, nothing—therefore, the mainline is the line of contact. It begins earlier than all; it ends later than all.

Since it is precisely we who are interested in establishing contact, we are doing everything to make it appear and be present throughout the communication. We find time for a meeting, we call up, we try to be noticed, and we dress and talk so that we are agreed to be distinguished from the general background—and even when a person "escapes" from communication, he thinks, "Is it not that I run too fast?"

Any advertisement should contain "contact information," the one on which the proposed product or service can be found—at least, with the help of a search engine.

If the advertisement is new-fangled and contact information has not yet been offered, it means that the seller prefers to keep in touch with you through his advertising media. A telephone and address will be offered later. This also corresponds to the structure.

Conversely, when a person is afraid that the impact of the other side will be more effective than his, he can just break the contact—so debtors avoid meeting with creditors, so passers-by try to get around street vendors and gypsies, so many business people refuse to watch TV, so children run away from home to not be invited to dinner, so weak fighters try to escape from the enemy, running around the edge of the tatami.

However, contact is not only important for this. Through the contact line, we receive information about the interlocutor's reaction to our influences: feedback. And based on this information, we correct our behaviour. Actually, this is one of the main differences between a literate communicator and an ordinary communicator—a literate one notices when he is mistaken and quickly fixes what needs to be fixed.

What the interlocutor likes, what he agrees with, what worries him, what he hides—he will tell us everything—not a word, so a body. Generally speaking, our line of contact pertains to the line of influence of the interlocutor on us. The words of the interlocutor give us the key to how to communicate with him—appearance, emotional reactions, the appearance or disappearance of signs of trance, changes in his posture and breathing—*open only your eyes and ears!*

Distraction Line

A man is designed so that his first involuntary reaction to a direct offer or request is a refusal—anyway, any new information. Outwardly, he may not give a look, but he is internally tense. (Track, by the way, your reaction to these allegations) Did you agree at once?) Then, after thinking and weighing the pros and cons, he can make a positive decision—but inexperienced communicators by this time May already leave upset.

We all unconsciously strive for the same thing—to maintain the status quo, so that nothing changes, to make everything familiar, and so that there were guarantees that tomorrow would be like yesterday—because we are already used to what we have. Let us live in a swamp, but it is ours and is familiar to the last bump. Here, we can easily get rid of any enemy—but we won't fight back, so we'll hide in a pre-prepared assortment. Therefore, the reaction to change is appropriate—*wary*.

And all this goes by the mind—involuntarily—that is, quite reasonable, logical, profitable ideas and suggestions pass by. In the sense of being eliminated, it is rejected at distant approaches. And few are able, having thought it all over again, to return to what he himself had sifted out. Therefore, even when we offer a person a truly valuable transaction, point of view, or information, we have to introduce a line of distraction.

In other words, in order to act effectively, it is necessary to distract the "internal controller" of the interlocutor. Well, about the same as if you wanted to get into a guarded building—you first have to deal with his guard. Say the password, show the pass, arrange for him a "call from above," sell to pity, bribe him, shy away with a baton, or blow up an explosion packet at a neighbouring entrance, finally. In a word, it is reliable to neutralize until we finish all the machinations we need.

How do you distract the "controller"? For example, the interlocutor's consciousness goes on a mental journey through the past or future, which we will arrange for him. Do you remember the charm of the words, "Do you remember," and the stories of, "Beautiful far away?" Likewise, let the "controller" get carried away with the struggle with the flow of information, fall into an emotional whirlwind, live in a fabulous reality, and listen to our explanations. (All this and much more are ways of inducing a conversational trance.) Let him be distracted. Because while he is watching, we cannot do anything worthwhile In the meantime, the "controller" is resting—we will work—and keep in touch with this!

Line of Exposure

When there is contact or when the interlocutor's consciousness is reliably distracted, a line of influence may appear—fragmentarily, imperceptibly, and always ready to hide even more reliably. On this line, we inspire—throw ideas, form the necessary attitude, suggest suitable interpretations motivate, awaken desires—*the main work is on-going.*

It is clear that the vast majority of suggestions are indirect. Yes, we are not impudent. We act just where we are not resisted. We do not suggest, "Give us all the money." We explain, "It's not just a cactus but a big-money cactus," and therefore, this cactus costs "only five thousand American dollars." We are not saying that the person needs to obey everything; we only make it clear that in the prevailing— *terrible!*

And I remind you: the line of action is fragmented. Most of our words are either reliable or unverifiable in the current conditions. However, our suggestions are forwarded: there is a not quite logical combination, and there is not a completely substantiated statement. Here, we say "possible," and after a couple of sentences, "only possible." Here, the word in one sense; there, in another. Likewise, for example, you can create a mood with one story, and then transfer it (there are special methods) to another—and all this briefly, forwarding, no pauses, continuing to speak, without stopping the speech flow, taking away attention away from "slippery places."

The second feature—all forwarding work for the same purpose, inspire the same thoughts—let the wording be different, but their essence is one. Thus, an outwardly ordinary conversation with all the usual paraphernalia turns out to be filled with a dense stream of suggestions that work for a given purpose.

At this moment, all three lines are simultaneously involved: impact, distraction, and contact—but *that* is the essence of a single impact structure.

Stages of Exposure

If you need to know about the three lines of communication necessary for success in order to understand the essence of a single impact structure, for practical use, it is useful to consider it as a sequence of stages, each of which is necessary and sufficient in its place.

How to move from lines to stages? It's very simple. If you project the background lines on top of each other, it turns out that there are five key segments in a single impact structure:

- Fixation of attention

- Depotentialization of control

- Intervention

- Latent period

- Synchronization

The presence of each of them is mandatory. The absence of any of them can ruin the effect on the root—and it is clear that, without finishing the previous one, it is impossible to move on soon enough. However, now, the difficult task of holding two or three background lines at the same time turns into a clear step-by-step scheme, from which it is clear what to do and why.

Fixation of Attention

Attraction and retention of attention—without it, no impact on a person is possible. For if you did not attract his attention, you, for him, are not—and nothing can affect. Therefore, the first active step in any manipulation algorithm is to fix attention.

Hence, the goal of the stage is to attract and capture the attention of a potential interlocutor so that it turns from potential into reality. To begin with, you provide yourself with the opportunity to be seen and heard. In order to do this, you can:

- Be in plain sight;

- Appear in a personal area (approximately 1.5 meters from the body);

- Say hello;

- Contact by name;

- Offer to talk;

- Offer to look at what you show;

- Ask for a moment of attention;

- Sometimes, touch;

- And so on.

However, it is not enough to attract attention—it is also necessary to *keep it*.

The attraction of attention is similar to wrestling capture—after it, reception is possible—and experienced fighters, by the way, are fighting precisely for the seizure, as the rest is a matter of technology. Then, you can make a trance, "powder your brain," and offer the interpretations we need. There is attention; they listen to you.

Attention must be attracted—and attracted attention must be retained (and in case of distraction, returned). In other words, to be effective, you must be able to attract attention constantly, over a given period of time, and then let go, and become invisible—you need to be able to do this, too.

Chapter 25 Covert Emotional Manipulation

N ow you are probably thinking is that different from Emotional Manipulation and if so, how. The answer is Emotional Manipulation occurs within the realms of your consciousness, so you are aware that someone is trying to appeal to a more generous side of you to get what they want. Think about the time when your parents wanted you to visit them for the summer but you had a different probably more exciting summer plans with your friends or a special someone and your parents insisted you visit them instead or take some extra time off to make the visit. You tried to convince them that you would visit for Thanksgiving and your calendar is booked solid and they might have retorted with statements like "we are old and we wouldn't be around for so long, you need to make us your priority" or "we haven't seen you in forever and we miss you, come over to visit your loving parents". During this conversation you are completely aware that your parents are attempting to change how you feel about your summer plans in their favor. This is a classic and harmless case of Emotional Manipulation. On the other hand, Covert Emotional Manipulation is carried out by individuals who are trying to gain influence over your thought process and feelings, with the means of subtle underhanded tactics that go undetected by the person being manipulated.

By definition Covert Emotional Manipulation goes undetected and leaves you acting like a pawn in the hands of the manipulator, which makes this a manifestation of Dark Psychology. The dictionary definition of the word covert is "not openly shown or engaged in"; therefore, it presents a stark difference from all other Emotional Manipulation techniques. The victims of Covert Emotional Manipulation are unable to understand the intent or motivation of the manipulator and the way they are being manipulation and even just the fact that they are being manipulated. Think of Covert Emotional Manipulation as a bomber with impeccable stealth, one that can tip toe in your subconscious without being detected, leaving you with no defense what so ever. Our emotions primarily dictate all other aspects of our personality and thus they also dictate our reality. Someone attempting to manipulate your emotions is equivalent to them cutting open your jugular vein making you lose control over yourself and your reality.

Let's have a brief look at some of the more frequently observed forms of dark manipulation.

Gas lighting

The tactic used by manipulators aimed at making their victim doubt their own thoughts and feelings is called Gas lighting. This term is often used by mental health professionals to describe the manipulative behavior to convince the victim into thinking their thoughts and feelings are off base and not in alignment with the situation at hand.

Passive-Aggressive behavior

Manipulators can adopt this duplicitous behavior to criticize, change behavior of their victim without making direct requests or aggressive gestures. Some of these traits include: sulking or giving the silent treatment, portraying them as a victim or intentionally cryptic speech.

Withholding information

There is no such thing as a white lie but manipulators often provide selective information to their victim, so as to guide them into their web of deception.

Isolation

Dark manipulator is always aiming to gain control and authority on their victim. In order to succeed they will create an increasingly isolated environment for their victim and prevent them from contacting their friends and family.

The many differences between Persuasion and Manipulation

1. Motive/Intent

As we have established people with active dark psychological traits including manipulators, aim to establish control and authority on their prey and exploit their victims to serve their own interests. On the other hand, persuaders are concerned about the wellbeing of their audience and attempt to convince them to change their attitude or behavior in a free environment.

2. Method of Delivery

Manipulators create an inviting environment for their victim, who is often an unwilling prey and primed emotionally and psychologically to act in ways that benefit their predators and threatens their own health or well-being. Whereas, persuaders only hope that their audience will respond to their influence and the suggestions. Ultimately the individual is free to decide whether or not they want to accept the suggestions made by their persuader and alter their thoughts, feelings and/or behaviors.

3. Impact on the social interaction

Dark manipulators will always aim to isolate their prey from the rest of the world and prevent any contact from their loved ones. The victim of dark manipulation like brainwashing, develop extreme views and may commit heinous acts of antisocial behavior. Unlike manipulation, acts of persuasion are never lethal for the audience and the society. It could be as harmless as your brother's admiration for Nike shoes leading you to buy a pair of your own or the ads from McDonalds inviting you to enjoy a quick meal with your family.

4. Final outcome

Persuasion usually results in one of these three possible scenarios: Benefit to both the persuaded and the persuader, commonly known as a win-win situation; Benefit only to the persuaded; Benefit to the persuaded and a third party. However, dark manipulation always has a singular benefactor that is the manipulator. The manipulated individual is at grave disadvantage and will act against their self-interest.

Chapter 26 Subliminal Psychology

Subliminal psychology, then, refers to how individuals can influence each other through subliminal methods. Think of subliminal as pertaining to the unconscious mind—the subliminal messages used are directly communicating with the unconscious mind in ways that largely fly underneath the radar of the conscious mind. In essence, it is all of the signals being sent to and understood by the unconscious mind that bypass the conscious mind's notice. These can be things that you are unaware of being present— faint scents in the air that you may not recognize or notice, but your unconscious does. It could be the way someone approaches aggressively, triggering an instantaneous defensive reaction as you prepare. It could be certain sounds or barely perceivable movements. No matter what it is, however, it is important to recognize as an incredibly powerful force in swaying others.

Subliminal psychology is all about remaining unnoticed. When using it on someone else, it must remain largely unnoticeable, quietly influencing the other person's thoughts and feelings in order to sway them into behaving a certain way. While their subconscious is aware of your influence, the conscious mind, on the other hand, remains largely in the dark. It is essentially a higher level of influence—through your knowledge of the situation and the workings of another's mind, you are able to carefully and covertly sway someone into behaving in ways that you want. You are able to sway situations with ease, and because it is largely unconscious, you should be able to utilize these skills with almost anyone, regardless of the context. It can enable you to persuade others that you are giving them control while still secretly maintaining the vast majority of it.

Emotions

Emotions are largely unconscious—they are what you feel in response to whatever is happening around you. They are your brain's attempt to translate your surroundings into a language your body can understand and react to. If you were to define emotions at their most fundamental level, they are states of mind you enter that are entirely reflexive, triggered by your response to the world around you. When your senses receive sensory input from the world, they are able to translate it into impulses that your body then feels. These impulses are your emotions—you feel the urge to do certain things in response, and those certain things are intended to be beneficial to you.

When you feel an emotion, it is because the emotion is supposed to help you somehow. In nature, before people were more or less insulated from the effects of the wild, these emotions would spur us to engage in survival instincts—we would feel more on edge when feeling as though there is a threat present, or feeling aggressive if we felt like our boundaries were being stepped on or that we were being wronged in some way. Happiness is a pleasant state and encourages you to constantly strive to be in it, cueing you that you have done something right.

These emotions keep you alive, and they aid in decision making as well. When behaving emotionally, you are foregoing the logical decisions and engaging in survival behaviors. You are intentionally making it a point to survive in any way possible, but that also typically results in behaving in ways that society may frown upon.

Now, think of the implications behind the concepts of emotions—emotions control behavior. If you can control emotions, you can then control behavior. What controls emotions? Physical stimuli in the world around the individual you are seeking to control.

This means that you can essentially control someone else through taking control of their surroundings. You can change what is happening around the other person. You can choose to treat the other person in a specific way to sway them into feeling a specific emotion. You can make something happen around the other person that will influence their feelings. Since feelings occur in response to the world around you, you can change that. You can directly interact with the world around someone else, meaning you can directly influence the other person's behaviors if you understand how to do so.

The most basic of emotions are the following:

·   Anger: Felt in response to boundaries being infringed upon or to protect one

·   Contempt: Felt when vehemently disagreeing and disliking someone or something—similar to hate

·   Disgust: Felt when something is toxic to your health or wellbeing

·   Anxiety or fear: Felt when convinced there is an imminent danger to one's health or life

·   Joy: Felt when everything is okay at that moment

·   Sadness: Felt when there has been loss or harm

·   Surprise: Felt when there is something unexpected happening

Needs

Living beings need several different things just in order to survive. We are complicated creatures—ultimately, we must meet several criteria to ensure that we are able to stay alive. At the most fundamental levels, people have a need for oxygen, food, water, warmth, and rest to survive, with sex also being considered a primary need as well. Humans will constantly be seeking out those six needs throughout their life. If these needs are not met or are infringed upon in some way, people grow more volatile and more desperate. People will begin to do things that are not socially acceptable just to ensure those needs are met.

When you are able to keep those needs in mind, you gain more control over other people. People who are not meeting those needs are not going to be able to focus nearly as well as those who have all of their needs met. Those who have met all of their needs are able to focus on rationality, thinking, and generally making choices for themselves. They have the energy and motivation to consider what is going on around them without fearing whether they will survive. Because they are not in some sort of survival mode, they can be in critical thinking mode instead.

Look at the six needs listed—each of them can be distracting in some way. If you are constantly hungry, your hunger will get worse. You will grow weak, and be unable to focus as your body diverts resources to keeping itself functional rather than to rational thought or higher thinking. If you are not able to breathe, you are going to be panicking and really only conscious for a short period of time, which is not exactly conducive to rational thoughts. If you are desperately thirsty and dehydrated, you will be too focused on locating water to survive. If you are freezing cold, you will be searching out the warmth and be desperate to do whatever it takes to find it. Your needs are designed to distract you—if they are not being met, your body needs to meet them as soon as possible in order to ensure your survival, and it knows that. It will drive you to survive because if you do not survive, you cannot pass on your genetic material, which is overall, the driving force behind nature as a whole.

When attempting to control someone else, this has serious implications as well— if you know someone has a need that has to be met, you can use subliminal messages that are tailored to that need. If someone is thirsty, for example, you can utilize subliminal messages to encourage the individual to buy a specific brand of a drink. If they are hungry, flashing messages about popcorn could actually potentially sway them to buy some.

Likes

For people, we tend to gravitate toward certain people, and when we like those people, we are far more receptive to persuasion and influence from those people. This means that in order to have that influence you may be seeking out; you need to ensure that you are likable. When you are, people will be more likely to follow you. Your subliminal messages are more likely to take, and you are more likely to get the results you desire. In order to make yourself likable, you need to do the following:

· Be relatable: If you can make yourself relatable in some way, the other person is bound to like you more. When they like you more, they want to do more things to keep you happy. You can attempt to appeal to this one through talking about yourself a little bit in interactions or doing other things that can make you more human in the minds of the other person.

· Pay compliments: By complimenting someone, you are essentially priming them. You are putting them into a good mindset, which you can then utilize later on in order to sway someone to do what it is that you need from them. The key here is that the compliments should be legitimate. If you are going to attempt to use them, you should mean what you are saying.

· Be cooperative: When you make it clear that you are interested in doing something that you both want, showing that you share a goal, the other person is far more likely to believe that you are sincere in your suggestions, granting you far more influence.

Making someone like an item is pretty similar, except instead of being relatable, you want the individual to relate to the target audience. If your peers like something, you are likely to like it. If it is something genuinely pleasant or that makes you feel good in some way, such as a food that brought you joy, or a shirt that you think looks good on you, you are essentially being complimented—you feel good after using the item. If the item is beneficial to you and makes your life easier, you see it as being useful, which is what someone is when they are cooperating with you.

Someone is going to be far more willing and receptive to subliminal psychology if they like whatever the message is trying to convince them to do. The process will be easier, and quite possibly more effective if the end result is something that the person likes or naturally wants simply because he or she likes it.

Chapter 27 How To Master The Basics Of Psychology

I f everyone around you is using tactics to get what they want, you may be tempted to want to do it at least once. But then, do you know how? Some of the tactics are things we may do occasionally but doing it deliberately and calculatedly can help us gain some amount of control over other people. Let us look at some of the ways that manipulators can apply dark tactics.

1. Hiding intentions

One form of manipulation that has been around since the beginning of time is lying. Manipulators usually use this tactic when they are faced with a responsibility that they want to flee from or when they feel that saying the truth will not benefit them. Many of them even go ahead to lie when they have no reason at all to do so and it makes them feel good to know that they are causing trouble and playing with others' feelings. When you come in contact with a skilled manipulator, they could make you believe in a lie until you're neck-deep in it. They may do this because they want to take advantage of someone else or they might just be using the lie as a smokescreen to cover their true intentions. Or they may be using it to prevent you from seeing that they want to keep being steps ahead of you.

For example, a friend who is looking for the same thing as you will hide any information that will make you get it before them.

2. Attention Seeking

Drama queen Drama King. We've probably had to use these words on people who are always being dramatic. It's not bad for one to have drama once in a while because life doesn't have to be too serious but manipulators thrive on frequent drama. They normally create it

147

intentionally because they want to be the center of attention and massage their ego.

For instance, in a group of three friends, one of them may try to cause conflict between friends A and B by peddling stories of each of them to the other party. This will make friends A and B to have misunderstandings and normally they will turn to the manipulator to lay their grievances and seek comfort. Because of this, the manipulator feels needed and important. One partner in a relationship can keep bringing up fights so that their partner will keep their attention on them.

3. Giving Off Unnecessary Emotions

Manipulators could be people who show emotions a lot, do dramatic stuff and have loud outbursts when they want to get their way. They are often loud, melodramatic and will go all emotional even at the slightest incitement and usually, they display their attitude in appropriate environments.

For instance, one partner may resort to raising their voice and arguing loudly in a restaurant because their partner is not giving in to their demands because they feel that their partner will be embarrassed by the scene and give in to what they want. This is a subtle and very effective manipulation tactic.

4. Crying Foul and Playing the Victim

There are people who love it when people feel sorry for them always. They are always making people feel that they have the worst of luck. They are the ones who will even make you feel guilty for complaining about your problems because they always have worse problems than yours. Of course, we all have bad moments but a manipulator knows how to make they look like the victim of all victims and draw lots of attention to themselves. Tell them you have a fever and they'll narrate to you how they've had to deal with migraines every day for the past month. Say you forgot your coffee cup and they'll tell you how their expensive coffee maker got destroyed. They just look for ways to solicit pity from people just so they can get attention and people's concentration.

5. Claiming Undue Credit

Manipulators do not see anything wrong in getting someone else to make the effort involved in something and then coming in, later on, to take credit for the work as if they have done a major part of the job. This kind of manipulation can be seen in a professional setting where people will be delegated to do jobs as a group but end up prancing around, being busy without actually doing anything and when the job is done, they come in to take credit for it.

6. They Want You to Depend On Them

Manipulators want to feel needed and they want you to need them. They want to see you agree that you cannot exist without them. In every social setting, you see them as the famous ones that attract and magnets others and it makes you feel like you should really be a part of them. That's what they thrive on.

A manipulative person in a relationship will always want to remind their partners that they are nothing without them and they cannot survive without them. They will do you a favor at your needy moment and create that feeling of indebtedness in you so that they will later come and ask you to return the favor. You cannot get a free favor from a manipulator.

Manipulators have built a fantasy that you need them in your life because as you continue to depend on them, their control over you grows and that is the main motive behind whatever help they are rendering to you. They come when you're vulnerable and they become indispensable and continue to enjoy the status that they have given themselves in your life. The more support they give you, the more their chances of leeching on to your emotions and taking advantage of you.

7. Selective Honesty

You may have experienced a complete betrayal from someone who seemed so generous and then after realizing that you didn't even know half of what was taking place, you felt awful. When a manipulator is feeding you with information, they will tell you only what they want you to know and intentionally hold back the rest and that is why you will feel terrible when you find out.

Using selective honesty to disarm unsuspecting people is a manipulative tactic that most professional settings make use of. If there is a promotion to compete for in a workplace, a manipulative colleague may keep feeding you information on the state of affairs. You might be thinking they care so much as to let you in on the inside info that they get without knowing that they are not telling you everything.

They may keep the juicy tip and hand to you whatever information they want to tell you while making you feel gratitude for their generosity.

8. Faux friendship

Some people could pretend to be friendly to you just because of their sinister motive. They could be acting like your friends while they are underground collecting every kind of information that they can about you. Although some people may be trying to be your friends but you should be careful if you are being asked personal questions especially when you are just meeting.

This tactic is often used in professional settings. Among friends too, there can be a friend who really tries to control the conversation without making it obvious. The conversation will be based on what they want; things will be done at their own pace. They could even manipulate you into taking impromptu decisions and that matter too.

9. Commitment issues

They have a lot of problems trying to commit to something. It doesn't even matter if you have asked for their support to do something important and urgent. They will find a way to hold back the response to your plea especially if it will put them in a place of power where they can turn the situation for their own benefit.

They only care about themselves and so you cannot see them commit to anything unless they will do it so they can have something to control you with.

10. Playing Dumb

You may see someone feigning innocence over something that is happening. Sometimes, they know more than they let on and they act as though they don't. People often overlook this manipulative tactic but it is mostly used in professional settings. In an office, an employee who may know something in full details may lie that they are not sure of what they know. The work will then be reassigned to someone else. Think about the times you have had misunderstandings in your group of friends. It is possible that the person who acts as though they know nothing about what led to the misunderstanding will get away with the fact that nobody knows how much information that have about why the disagreement happened.

11. Pointing a finger at others

You will never find a manipulator with dirt on their record. They strive to make sure nothing is found on them by keeping their hands clean

They do this by staying away from all forms of responsibility and also by accusing someone whenever there is a problem, so they can easily wriggle out of whatever it is. You will notice this especially when the issue is something that can tear their reputation apart and make people see them for their lies and deceit. A manipulator is the person around you that blames everybody else for a problem but themselves. To them, they are never a problem and will often want someone else to be their scapegoat.

12. Saying what you want to hear

When you're being flattered, you feel good. It's difficult to not feel flattered and you will start making conscious effort to like the person that is saying the things that you always want to hear. Of course, we will be drawn towards being with these people who are always saying what will be pleasant to our hearing. Despite how good you feel about hearing those things, it doesn't show that you're with a good friend. Besides, they could just be massaging your ego and soliciting your love for when they will want a bigger favor and you will be tempted to grant it to them because you feel that they have been so good to you.

13. Controlling decisions

You can see manipulation in a romantic relationship when one partner tries to control the other party's decision.

It is very normal for someone in a relationship to want to make their decisions based on their partner but the motive behind it is what matters. Is the decision made to truly make them delighted or are you trying to avoid their wrath?

In a relationship, there is just a thin line between making a partner happy and manipulation.

When you find yourself canceling many plans too often because of the way your partner feels or you stop putting on some outfits that you like, or cut your hair or do something's just because of your partner. Then there is a possibility that they are controlling your life on a low key. It may start off with innocent and harmful suggestions but in the long run, you will find out that you're only living to please and you're doing only little to make yourself happy.

Conclusion

Congratulations on making it throughout the book. You might still need some practice or have to do further research in specified areas, but you should still feel really proud of where you are now. There are so many people in this life that will blindly follow others. There are many individuals that will never look deep within themselves and really confront your thoughts. It's not easy to do so, but it's important that we really dive deep into our psyche in order to live a happier and healthier life.

Remember that it's still perfectly normal and healthy to let others influence you! Think of all the great leaders of the world and how they might be able to inspire positive passion and inspiration in those that follow them. You are not wrong for falling under the influence of others. The difference going forward is that it's going to be based around positive and uplifting inspiration rather than malicious-intentioned manipulation.

Always remember as you travel throughout your life that you need to use your brain power for good. Even though it might be hard sometimes, this is always going to be the better option. You might find yourself in a position one day where you have a very simple and reachable chance to manipulate someone else. Don't take advantage of this! The other person might be someone easily manipulated, and maybe on some level it is their own fault for not being more aware. Never assume this, however! Some individuals will have gone through things that really made it harder for them to break free from their thinking patterns and discover a healthier method of dealing with their thoughts and feelings.

Always help others, never hurt them. Even those that might have done the same to you in the past shouldn't be individuals that you target.

You are an intelligent person who can use their powers for good. Make the world a better place with healthy influence and you will discover that this brings you everything that you have ever wanted.

This book was to prepare you for the world of dark psychology better. We are all part of the world that has tendencies to have some very dark people on it. It is important to look out for yourself when it comes to building new relationships and friendships. We have pretty much laid out how you should know if you are being manipulated and ways to get out of it. If you are still unsure if you are being manipulated, share some of your stories with friends or family members. You should even share it with a trusted doctor or therapist. With all of these people in your life, you should be able to see what your relationship is doing to your life finally. Just think about how much happier you will be when you make a good decision to get out of your abusive and manipulative relationship. You will be free of the negative energy in your life, and you will be able to begin again and move onto a much greener pasture in the end. Stick with your final decision to leave this abusive life and start a brand new one. Remember that you are completely worth it, and you will be able to find the ways to make yourself happy without someone trying to control your entire life and making you incredibly unhappy. Just remember to look for the traits and signs of those who have manipulated in the past. You are well on your way to living a happier life once you finish this book.